BLUEPRINT
for
congregational
youth
ministry

WITHDRAWN

by Lavon J. Welty

Foreword by
Barbara Varenhorst

Faith and Life Press
Newton, Kansas

Mennonite Publishing House
Scottdale, Pennsylvania

DEDICATION

To Andrea and Renetta—who have shown me most clearly how it is to be an adolescent in the 1980s.

PREFACE

In many respects this book is an attempt to bring together what I have learned about ministry with youth in the congregation over the past decade. It is, furthermore, an effort to develop a broad framework for youth ministry in congregations that have a particular understanding of faith, that of a "believers' church" perspective.

Blueprint for Congregational Youth Ministry is a project of the Integrated Congregational Youth Ministry Council, a group of youth workers from the Church of the Brethren, General Conference Mennonite Church, and the Mennonite Church. They meet regularly to discuss materials and issues related to youth ministries in their denomination. The Council's goal is to create subsequent volumes (resources) related to youth ministry concerns. The next project that is planned is a guide for mentoring.

Blueprint for Congregational Youth Ministry is a foundational piece for the youth ministry library. It is not a "how to" book in the sense of outlining a variety of actual programs. It is rather a "why" book, describing the needs of individual young persons and what the congregation can do to meet those needs.

Blueprint for Congregational Youth Ministry is a handbook for people who care about and walk with youth. Its uniqueness lies in the emphasis on individual emergence in the context of a caring, committed congregation. This book will be valuable to the community of faith which seeks to design a holistic plan for ministry with youth.

Many persons have taught me in my pilgrimage in ministry with youth. I would note in particular Robert Zuercher, who was my predecessor in the youth ministries office at the Mennonite Board of Congregational Ministries, the denominational office of the Mennonite Church. Bob expanded my thinking to see the importance of meaningful, supportive relationships between youth and adults in the congregation, and demonstrated to me the need for some new directions beyond the peer group setting in congregational youth ministries.

I am grateful for the influence of my colleagues in the youth ministry offices of the two denominations that have cooperated in making this book possible. Paula Diller Lehman of the General Conference Mennonite Church and Christine Michael of the Church of the Brethren have been especially helpful in providing encouragement as well as helpful nudges to expand my awareness in this important area. Similarly, those who have touched my life from their role in youth ministry in the provincial and district conferences have also taught me a great deal. Perhaps more than anyone else, John Rogers of the Congregational Literature Division of the Mennonite Publishing House raised pertinent—sometimes vexing—questions that always helped me clarify my thinking and writing.

Many others from the broader Christian church have also been my teachers. Among these I would mention only two. The first is Michael Warren, whose book *Youth and the Future of the Church*, first helped me to understand that youth in Western culture are among the most oppressed people in society. He convinced me that the church can empower youth to true freedom. The influence of his book, as well as his subsequent writings on youth ministry, pervades the early chapters of this book. I gratefully acknowledge his influence.

The second person is Barbara Varenhorst, who introduced me to peer counseling as she developed it for implementation in the public schools. Varenhorst, a school psychologist, pioneered this concept and has seen it used and adapted in many schools across North America. She has unselfishly encouraged its use in congregational youth ministry as well. Many of the ideas in the section on peer ministries in chapter 9 were learned from conversations with her, her writings on the subject, and several presentations that I was privileged to hear.

I am also grateful to the General Conference Mennonite Church Commission on Education, to Mennonite Publishing House, and especially to the Mennonite Board of Congregational Ministries for financing this project and for allowing me staff time to write.

Finally, I would express appreciation to my wife, Carol, who hung in there with me when I doubted my own capabilities to communicate clearly those things that I have come to believe so strongly about ministry with the young persons of our congregations.

Lavon Welty

FOREWORD

All of my professional life has been devoted to working with youth, primarily in public schools, but also in the church. Over these years, I have agonized about the poor quality of youth programs within the church—the limited vision of what youth want and need; the limited depth of programming and curriculums; the minimal status on the church budget, if included at all; the hassling and pleading to find *someone* to be in charge of the activities which do exist; and the under-utilization or token status accorded youth within the church. Knowing that youth are our resources for the future, I firmly believe that the church must take the lead and model the stewardship of helping young people be and become the people God has meant them to be.

Because of this conviction and vision, I found Lavon Welty's *Blueprint for Congregational Youth Ministry* exciting and significant. This is not a critique of what isn't or hasn't been, or a list of problems. Rather, it is an extremely positive and workable overview of what youth ministry should and can be. Those who read and study this book will discover a clear and comprehensive understanding of youth ministry, including practical information about how to proceed in building or rebuilding a new, vital structure of youth ministry in their congregations. I also believe that readers will experience fresh motivation and commitment for seeing that this happens.

The blueprint itself, outlined in detail, with specific suggestions for implementation, is excellent. But much of its strength and validity comes from the foundation the author establishes in terms of beginning where young people are in their developmental process. As he explains the desire and need of young people to make decisions, and their search for significance, one is led to think of them as *people*—not a category for a particular type of program. Reminded of this, one can begin conceptualizing creative ways the church can serve and minister to them effectively.

The concept presented in the chapter on influencers and persuaders is very helpful and is critical. The issue presented is the key to why the church *must* be involved in youth ministry and why it must be implemented with exceptional care and excellence. However, the author is careful to point out that the church must not use its influence to indoctrinate, but rather to provide the environment within which young people can find their own faith, identity, and commitment. As a young person experiences this within a congregation and is provided with opportunities to express a faith commitment, the church is helping him or her find significance as an expression of God's love in the world.

A book on youth ministry should be vital and alive, conveying warmth, humanness, and love. This one does! Throughout its pages it sparkles with warmth and expresses concepts with powerful simplicity. Somehow, pointing out an adolescent's need to make decisions feels more human and real than expressing it as a "need to achieve autonomy." Likewise, "influencers and persuaders" seems more rich than terms like "the power of the media," or "peer pressure." In my own work in Peer Ministry, I will use many times the simple, but memorable, definition of youth ministry Lavon has given us: "that which is helping young persons *be* and *become* expressions of God's love in their world."

Lavon Welty, through this book, has become a persuader of the excitement of youth ministry and the challenge it presents. He has also restored my faith that the church *can* and desires to serve youth within the church, so that youth can, indeed, become the expressions of God's love in the world.

—*Barbara Varenhorst*

CONTENTS

Chapter 1: BLUEPRINT: a plan for building youth and program

The first two parts of this book form the foundation of the structure we seek to build. Part III describes the super-structure of a rebuilt youth ministry program in the congregation.

The huge banner across the front of the store proclaimed "Open for Business."

Eight months earlier the grocery store had been heavily damaged by fire. Even while the firefighters battled the blaze, the owners began to think about the major, difficult decisions that lay ahead of them. Should they tear down whatever remained and build completely new or should they salvage what was left? At first the easiest thing seemed to be to bulldoze the whole thing away and build completely new.

However, after the fire was out and the owners had taken a good look at what was left, rebuilding around what remained began to look just as good. The storefront was a landmark in the community and it appeared to be intact. To build around it would keep this familiar landmark. At the same time, they could add some new features which would serve their customers better.

Either option would require much study and thought. The owners decided to take a fresh look at the interests of their regular shoppers before doing anything else. They would need the information to make changes in their operation which would serve the customers better as well as attract new customers. Insurance agents, architects, contractors, and their banker all provided expert advice.

Today the store was buzzing with activity as familiar persons returned for the first time since the fire.

Youth ministry under fire

For the past decade youth ministry has also been under fire. In many congregations it has taken heat from parents who hurt when their sons and daughters lose interest in church activities, including the youth group which had been so important to those parents. Many youth state that church is boring. Youth ministry has also been under fire from some sponsors who refuse to serve more than one term and often cannot wait until that is finished.

If you mention youth ministry in many congregations, members almost immediately think of the youth group. Even though youth are present for other congregational activities, youth group is the only setting where members think ministry to young persons takes place. Furthermore, adults in the congregation have come to expect that youth group will be the primary church experience for youth. This has, in effect, made the youth group a parallel congregation. The youth group sponsors are often in the precarious position of being the bridge between the two.

We might visualize today's youth ministry and its relationship to the congregation like this:

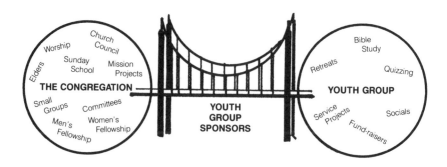

In some congregations, this youth-group-centered youth ministry meets their youths' needs quite effectively. But in many others, the youth group is struggling. Some are asking whether there is any point in trying to keep it going. The whole structure seems to be burning. It is very tempting to tear the whole thing down and begin again with something completely new.

Others try everything possible to make youth group what it once was. Leaders plan more social activities, all-day excursions to the beach or amusement park, or weekend retreats to make it more inviting and exciting. These, they hope, will attract youth and compete with all their other many and varied social activities. Or a charismatic, youthful youth minister is hired who will keep the youth interested with skillful guitar playing, bird-call imitations, and humor. The structure is burning or has already been destroyed. Major effort goes into rebuilding the youth group just as it once was.

A plan for rebuilding youth ministry

This book is a "blueprint" for rebuilding youth ministry in the congregation. In it we take our cues from the owners of our burned-down grocery store. They finally decided to retain the familiar storefront, rebuilding around it while adding a variety of features that would serve their customers more effectively. They did this, however, only after doing the more difficult work of gathering data about their community, analyzing it, and establishing direction for their continued service to their customers.

In developing a blueprint for congregational youth ministry it is tempting to think first about a program. But before thinking about program, leaders in youth ministry must think about the most fundamental concern, that is, *building the life of each young person.* Therefore, a truly useful blueprint must be based on understanding youth and what shapes them. It is just as important for the church to think clearly about what it wants to be in relation to its young people.

Youth ministry today is about persons created in God's image—persons for whom Christ died. It is helping young persons recognize that God is reaching out to them and wants to be in relationship with them, as they are. It is helping youth tune into God's way, and in commitment to Christ, helping them let God's love shine through them. In short, it is helping youth discover their own unique blueprint. Elizabeth O'Connor, in her book *Eighth Day of Creation* (Word Publishers, 1974), suggests:

A primary purpose of the Church is to help us discover our gifts and, in the face of our fears, to hold us accountable for them so that we can enter into the joy of creating. The major obligation of the Church to children is to enjoy them and to listen to them so that each can grow according to the design which is written into his being and emerges only under the care and warmth of another life. One of the reasons we experience so much difficulty with our gifts is that parents have thought their chief function in life to be feeding, clothing, and educating the young. However, their really important ministry is to listen to their children and enable them to uncover the special blueprint that is theirs.

The first two parts of this book form the foundation of the structure we seek to build. We will look more closely at who youth are and what the congregation can be as it ministers with them. Part III describes the superstructure of a rebuilt youth ministry program in the congregation. Some readers may wish to read this section first.

In this blueprint we recognize the vital role of the youth group in youth ministry. But we also recognize that there are various other settings in the congregation where the lives of youth are touched. Some of these have existed for many years but have not been recognized as part of youth ministry. Consequently, these have not been integrated or coordinated with the youth group. Others may be new. Some are settings where the youth come together as peers. Others are intergenerational, involving persons of all ages.

Such a rebuilt youth ministry can be visualized like this:

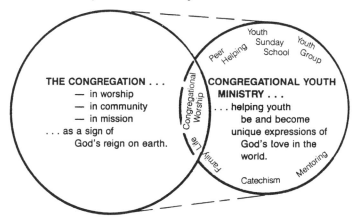

This picture sets youth ministry within the congregation—a vital part of its total life. It is a part of the congregation as it worships, builds community, and extends God's reign in mission, both in peer settings and with other age groups.

The diagram also shows seven settings in the congregation where the lives of youth are touched in direct, specific ways. The circle suggests that these must be seen as part of an integrated effort. Both the content and activities of each must be selected so that each complements the others and all are focused by the same vision and purpose, that of helping young persons be and become unique expressions of God's love in the world.

Before we examine the blueprint in greater depth, we must be clear about one thing. Some congregations would attempt to isolate and protect their youth from the "world" by their youth ministry. In this book we make the assumption that youth of the church exist in the world and therefore are confronted by many different voices to which they must respond. Their lives are complex and fast-paced. Youth ministry, therefore, is about *being* and *becoming*. The church must be their most important resource as they live and respond today. It must also prepare them for their future as they face the responsibilities of adulthood. What an exciting, dynamic task!

Part I: Youth

A place to start

Rebuilding congregational youth ministry must begin with youth themselves. Our greatest concern is to understand how each young person goes about building his or her identity and, ultimately, life itself. What assumptions and understandings shape the way adults in Western culture—including the church—think about and respond to youth in their personal project of building identity and life?

Our starting point, if we are to rebuild congregational youth ministry on firm ground, will be to acknowledge and view youth as decision makers in their own right. While in some cultures teenagers have many of their decisions made for them, in Western culture it is assumed that youth make most, if not all, of their own decisions. These decisions are the primary structural elements—the wood and the bricks—of their identity and life building project. The mortar that holds them together is the values, the convictions, and the beliefs on which they base their decisions.

Adolescence is a time when many decisions need to be made. It is also a time when youth become aware of many things that will need to be resolved at some time in the future. Young persons obviously do not make their decisions totally alone. Indeed, how they mix their mortar—their values, convictions, and beliefs—is related to their deepest longings. We look at this in terms of a search for significance.

Mixing this mortar is of great interest to many persons and groups who would want to influence and persuade them. The motives of these influencers and persuaders are not always pure or in the best interests of the youth.

We can freely admit that the church is one of the influencers and persuaders that has interest in how youth shape their identities and build their lives. Too often it has copied the approaches of those influencers and persuaders who do not care as much about youth as persons as about themselves and their own interests. The larger task of our work in this book is to ask how the church in its youth ministry can be of greatest and best help to youth as each one shapes identity and builds life. To do so requires a rebuilding of how we have come to do youth ministry. Parts II and III provide a "blueprint" for this important project.

Chapter 2: YOUTH ARE DECISION MAKERS: forming an identity

Our starting point will be to acknowledge and view youth as decision makers in their own right. These decisions are the primary structural elements—the wood and the bricks—of their identity and life-building project.

Deciding alone with help

Several years ago I spent considerable time with my daughter as she worked through an important decision. We, as her parents, had given her the opportunity to attend our church-sponsored high school. She had to decide whether to remain in the public school or transfer.

She talked at length with friends about this decision. She also talked with teachers from both schools and with her mentor—an adult friend from church. She wanted to know what we would like her to do. With each conversation she added to her lists of pros and cons of attending each school. She noted carefully how her interests would be served most effectively in each. She took very seriously the advice and counsel she received from others, including us, her parents. I relaxed because I saw the integrity of her process.

Through the whole process our daughter made it clear that she wanted this to be her decision. There were times I questioned whether she was capable of making the decision. We also knew that whatever she decided we would want to provide some supplemental experiences for her. However, it seemed that deciding on a school herself was very important for her at this particular time in her life. This was only one of many, many decisions that she was to make during her teenage years.

Decisions facing teenagers

Every stage in life is filled with many decisions. Yet adolescents are confronted with a host of decisions, many of which are of major importance.

Family life. Each individual makes a unique contribution to the group of persons called the family. Each person also draws energy from that group. Sometimes an adolescent will actually sap the family's energy and resources by the unwise decisions he or she makes.

- How will he choose to relate to parents and siblings?
- Will she cooperate willingly in household and family tasks?
- How will he choose to deal with parental authority and the need for independence?
- How will she respond to the values and attitudes that are important to her parents?
- In what ways will he relate to the family's traditions and history? Will he choose to accept it as his own or reject it?
- When will she decide to set up her own household and how will she deal with issues of separation?

Peer relationships. Teenagers often form friendships with persons their own age and have little or no opportunity to make friends with persons from other generations. Is anything more depressing than peer relationships that seem to be going badly or is anything more rewarding than when friendships are going well? Those who think they have few friends can feel a terrible loneliness.

- What qualities will she look for in her friends?
- Will he compromise his values and beliefs in order to be part of the crowd?

- How will she relate to peers who appear to be different, such as the handicapped, those less affluent or cultured, those of a different race, or those less capable intellectually?

Moral issues. A wide range of moral issues confront each teenager.
- How sexually active will he be? Will that include premarital sexual intercourse?
- Will she use alcoholic beverages and tobacco?
- What will his attitudes towards persons of other races and cultures be?
- What values will guide her attitudes and behaviors toward the natural environment and material possessions?

The church and faith. The decisions that young persons make individually and as a group make a great deal of difference in the life of the church. Indeed, the presence of youth can do much to shape a congregation.
- Will he choose to be an active participant in the life of the congregation?
- Will she choose to commit herself to Christ and identify with the story of God's activity with the human race throughout history?
- Will church be something of an embarrassment to him or will he openly identify with it among his peers?
- How will she respond to emphases somewhat peculiar to her congregation or denomination, such as peace, justice, and nonresistance?
- How will he respond when it becomes evident that not all the members actively live out what the church teaches?
- In what ways will she apply the teachings of the church to her daily life?

Sexuality. Adolescence is a time of awakening sexuality. Many feelings and choices accompany this new awareness.

- What does it mean to be female or male?
- What attitudes and assumptions will the teen have concerning roles of the opposite sex? How will she respond to the stereotypes so prevalent for males and females in the media and surrounding culture?
- Will he be willing to make an effort to incorporate into his lifestyle those qualities not considered appropriate by his culture?
- How will she choose to relate to the opposite sex, in casual relationships or in dating?
- How will he deal with the strong physical urges that cry out for expression, and which are often stimulated by sexual innuendos and explicit scenes in commercials, in movies, or magazines?

Use of time. Most youth have much freedom in how they will use their time. Many find themselves with extremely busy schedules and little free time for themselves. An increasing number of young persons are having to resort to calendars and date books because of their full schedules.

- What priority will she give to schoolwork and extracurricular activities?
- How much time will he reserve for church, home, and family? In what community activities such as sports or clubs will he participate?
- When will she have time to be alone, to think, to dream, to reflect, or to worship in solitude? How much time will she give to physical fitness and other health concerns?
- Should he find part-time employment during the school year?
- What will be left out and who will feel left out when there simply is not enough time for everything? Or, if there seems to be too much time, how will she choose to use it?

Use of money. Many youth are employed. The money they earn gives them more freedom to purchase whatever they choose than they may ever have again, even as adults.

- What priorities will guide her in spending her money?
- Will he consider tithing and regular giving to the church?
- How much should she save for college, university, or other major future activities?
- Will he be concerned about major purchases like a car or stereo?
- How will she differentiate between needs and wants?
- How will he respond to other youth who have less money because they have chosen not to work or simply cannot find a job?

The future. Many questions about the future take on greater importance as the young person moves toward the end of high school.

- When will she leave home and establish her own household?
- How will he support himself?
- What interests and abilities, for possible long-term employment, can she develop with further training?
- Will he go to college or university after high school? If so, which college or university will he attend? Will it be a church school or a secular one?
- Will she marry, and if so, when? How will she decide on a life partner?
- What will be his basis for hope in the midst of a future that seems clouded by the possibility of a nuclear war?
- What will be her response should her country require its young persons to participate in war?

Worldview. Youth share this planet not only with other persons but also with the non-human environment—plants and animals and every other thing, living or not living.

- How will she relate to all the other peoples of the earth?
- What responsibility will he assume in caring for the natural world?
- What attitude will she have to the needs of future generations?

- What political goals and ideals will he adopt? Will these be basically self-centered and nationalistic? Or, will they include a desire for the well-being of all the people of the earth regardless of nationality, race, or culture?
- Is life essentially competitive or can she live successfully guided by a cooperative attitude? What will be her attitude toward the violence that exists in so many parts of society?

Support system. All of us require encouragement and support to maintain our way of living. The system that is developed to provide that encouragement and support will both shape and strengthen our convictions.
- How will parents, siblings, and extended family members be included in his support system?
- Will the support system be made up of a mix of persons from differing generations or primarily of peers her own age?
- What role will the church play in forming his support system?

Such a list of questions, though not exhaustive, helps us see what a truly awesome task youth face. While some decisions can wait (and some of them may never be fully resolved) until adulthood, many of them must be dealt with during the teen years. If they are not resolved, these years can be quite miserable. Furthermore, the young persons will hardly be prepared for what they will face in the adult years.

Identity shaping—Who am I? Who will I be?
During childhood, but even more during adolescence, individuals are developing their own store of information on which to base their decision making. As children they largely make decisions based on what they have seen in their parents. But as time goes on and they get more experience, they begin to put together their own beliefs, convictions, and values. There is intense interest in this process

by many different persons and groups. Youth also respond to their own inner needs in this process.

Shaping an identity is the sum of those decisions that finally answer the question: "Who am I and who will I be?" It is closely related to the biblical concept of the "heart." It thus includes the basic orientation that one takes in life, the values out of which one operates, and the faith commitment that one makes.

The study of human growth and development tells us that great strides are taken during the adolescent years in the basic formation of identity. Erik Erikson wrote extensively about this in his important book, *Childhood and Society* (1963), concluding that those who do not carry out this task successfully can develop a confused sense of role throughout their lives.

Shaping an identity is a lifelong process. Childhood experiences are important in this process but it becomes even more clearly focused in young persons as they take greater responsibility for their decision making. In this we often see them experimenting with differing ideals, behaviors, and involvements.

The fact is that these decisions come at a time when they are hardly prepared to face them. Consequently, their decision making is sometimes a process of trial and error. Fortunately, the outcome is often successful. Some trials bring praise. Others lead to criticism, reprimand, or punishment. All of these experiments can be important in the developing identity if they are appropriately interpreted. If not, the result can be a self-doubt and confusion that can further weaken an already fragile identity.

We can get a clue to how young persons are shaping their identity by observing their decisions. The decisions that young persons make are often the cause of great joy or deep pain for those who care about them. Such joy or pain can be caused by a single, isolated decision, but the deepest joy or concern comes from observing the decisions over a period of time. It is this longer view from which we can see consistent patterns emerging and in which we can observe the shaping of identity. Just as important in this is the process that the young person uses and the resources that he or she draws on to make the decisions.

Some will avoid making decisions as long as possible or simply do what their friends or parents say. With little ability to think on their own, they go along with what everyone else seems to be doing. Caught in a tight situation when they must make a decision quickly, they do what seems easiest or most natural in that situation.

For a few, the pressures and stress this causes are more than they are able to handle. Persons who observe the youth scene today note increasing numbers of youth who are depressed and experience a great deal of stress. There has been much publicity and alarm over the number of teenagers who are choosing suicide. As one young person stated, suicide seems to be the only answer, but what many do not understand is that it is a permanent answer to problems that in reality are temporary.

There are those youth, though sometimes it seems there are not very many, who do work through their decisions carefully. At the beginning of this chapter I described a decision that my daughter worked through carefully. I was very proud of her. We can be grateful for those youth who have developed good decision-making skills and can work deliberately with each decision that they face. While some may work through these decisions more quickly than others, these young persons have developed the ability to think clearly about the options, to discuss them with others who can help them see the advantages and disadvantages of each option, and then make a careful decision.

Frustrations and joys of parents and youth leaders
The adolescent years are a time of both *being* and *becoming*. In this being and becoming process, young people are constantly being confronted with and influenced by a vast range of options from which they choose the various parts that ultimately form their truly unique identity.

Parents and others who work with youth must understand this being and becoming process. One day a son or daughter may exhibit all those qualities that make a parent extremely proud. The parent is tempted to believe that maturity is finally beginning to shine through. But the next week the same son or daughter seems to have lost whatever maturity they had shown. The parent wonders what happened. Those who do not understand see the feeling of satisfaction felt a week earlier fade away. Parents again question whether their son or daughter has heard or understood anything that they have tried to communicate.

The decisions that youth sometimes make appear to have little or no logic or reason by adult standards. Take for instance the matter of "cruising"—driving up and down Main Street. Adults look at the wasted gas, the litter on the street the morning after, the possible illegal drugs and alcohol that may be a part of the scene. Most adults ask, "What fun can there be in that?"

But if you ask the teens who are part of it, they will say that they do it because *it is fun*. It is fun to see and be with friends as you drive up and down the street. And if there is a bit of rowdy behavior and loud music—that is part of the fun. And if there is littering—cleanliness is not everything; it can be picked up tomorrow.

Adults and youth—seeing things differently

And so the differences in the way things are seen go on and on.

- Adults want peace and quiet at night; night is when the fun begins for many youth.
- Adults believe that money wasted today means money not available for things in the future; youth freely spend what they have now because the present is what really matters.
- Adults like things orderly and neat; many youth seem most comfortable in their rooms when it looks like a tornado just passed through.

16

- Adults want to have all the facts before making a decision; youth tend to decide on the basis of feelings.
- Parents believe that a full closet means that there are enough clothes; youth feel that the clothes are out of style and may as well be given away.
- Youth sponsors at youth conventions can't understand how the young people can keep going on a very small amount of sleep; they believe the lack of sleep is a form of self-abuse. For the youth, sleeping interferes with fun and relationships and has a low priority; they will "catch up" next week.

Typical adult-leader reactions

Make decisions for them. Sometimes parents and others who work with youth are tempted to "take over" and make decisions they believe the young persons are not capable of making. It is at that time that the reminder comes: "I am fourteen (or eighteen or sixteen) and I am old enough to make my own decisions."

Veto or reverse a decision. There may be occasions when parents or other adults feel that they must step in and undo what has been decided or say no after the young person has said yes. Most youth will build resentment or anger if they are consistently denied the freedom to make their own decisions. Furthermore, when the time comes for them to be on their own and they must make their own decisions, they may be handicapped by the continuing control of parental authority, even if it is only in their mind. Or, they will make their decisions with a vengeance. They will reject everything their parents stood for as a way to get back at them.

These circumstances make clear the most important task in youth ministry: helping youth develop effective decision-making skills based solidly in an identity that is formed in a relationship with God through Jesus Christ, in being and becoming an expression of God's love in the world.

How can the church carry forward this important task?

Some will take a "hands-off" approach. Some adult leaders want to let the decision-making skills develop as they will. They look back at their own experience and believe that the questions facing today's youth are no different from their own experience a generation ago. We can have confidence, they think, because we made it, even if with varying degrees of success. Youth today will make it, too.

However, times have changed. Those who want to influence and persuade are making their pitch much more forcefully than ever before. Furthermore, there is far less support for youth in their decision making.

My peers and I looked primarily to our families and the church for clues for decision making. Often the expectations were very clear: we would not participate in activities parents thought were harmful or that the church frowned upon. Dances and movie theaters were out. We would attend church regularly, three times a week. We would not smoke cigarettes or drink alcoholic beverages. These expectations were deeply rooted in our parents' faith understandings. In many respects we were protected from evil influences.

We had to decide what we would do with the limitations given to us by parents and church. Some of us accepted those restrictions with little complaint, even though we may have envied other teens who seemed to be having so much fun doing things we could not do. Others became angry and rebellious, disregarding the expectations, no matter how much it hurt their parents.

Most parents today, however, know that it is no longer possible to protect their children as they were protected. Some of them have given up trying to influence or restrict their son's or daughter's activities even though they may not be very comfortable with the choices they make. Some parents even encourage participation in activities that they were not allowed as a way to express their own inner longing to have done these things.

18

Some will help youth develop skills. Many parents and youth leaders realize that the answers simply cannot be found as easily as before. Huge amounts of information, which come via television and other media, have to be considered in making most decisions today. Experiences that were never a part of the adult's life are stark realities in the youth's. Wise parents and leaders see the importance of helping youth in this information-saturated culture as they develop their decision-making skills.

Helping them develop such skills is not an easy task. It is made more difficult when we see that for many youth today the wisdom and experience of older persons is not as available as it was several decades ago. Then, as primarily a rural people, sons and daughters worked closely with parents doing the farm chores and gardening. Visits with grandparents and other extended family members were frequent. Other significant adult relationships beyond family were also part of the young person's experience as church was the primary social context.

Many families today, however, do not live close to other extended family members. For those who do, busy schedules make it difficult for families to get together other than on special occasions. In order to maintain their lifestyle, both parents are often employed, making them less available to their children. Furthermore, the teen's own busy schedule means much less time at home where parent-teen conversation can take place.

Some will help youth build a support system. In the face of the circumstances youth face in today's world, perhaps the most critical of the questions posed at the beginning of the chapter is that of their *support system.* The church must help each youth develop a support system that will be their primary resource for decision making.

- It must include both persons their own age and persons from other generations.
- It will help youth develop a "data base" of information from which to reflect on what the influencers and persuaders in the culture are saying.

- Such a support system will help youth understand that they do not have to make final choices for every decision by the time they finish high school. Decision making continues throughout life.
- It will also help them see that the decisions and directions set during the teen years are very important and may be difficult to reverse. Some decisions that appear to be unimportant on the surface may have more far-reaching effects than they might ever imagine. Many adults become aware of this when they have memories of their teen years they wish they could erase.
- A support system of caring persons can often help a young person find what is the right thing to do and also provide the needed courage and strength to do it.
- These caring "support persons" will also seek to remind the youth that true significance comes from being an expression of God's love in the world.

It is imperative that the church take seriously its responsibility in providing a place for young persons to develop their support system which will help them work through their many decisions. Sadly, many do not. Then, when a young person loses interest in the church, parents are faulted or those who work with youth are blamed.

Congregations do not intentionally avoid this responsibility. Leaders often simply do not keep abreast of the changing circumstances that face youth. Or, the congregation gets caught up in doing programming the way it always has been done. A change will require a rebuilding project, where the church looks first of all at itself and asks how it can provide a hospitable environment for youth. Then it will need to take a critical look at the programs it provides in its ministry with youth.

Chapter 3: SEARCHING FOR SIGNIFICANCE: the deepest longing of youth

Can the church reach out to youth, affirm them as valued persons, and help them construct a firm foundation on which they can base significance?

Cruising—a deeper meaning

Each evening, especially on the weekends, Main Street in my town is turned into a playground for teenagers, young adults, and a few older adults and their vehicles. They are cruising just to see what is happening. Many of the young persons are in family cars. Others are in "driving machines" with powerful motors capable of laying rubber a full city block. The huge, oversize tires give the drivers a view high above the rest. Deep red—or blue or green— metallic paint is polished to shine like a mirror and state-of-the-art stereos blare rock music mercilessly.

Those who live downtown view this cruising ritual with disgust. They say it is an invasion of their space, as it fills the air with the noise of squealing tires, roaring mufflers, and music that grates on their ears and nerves. The air is filled with exhaust fumes while streets are blocked, making it difficult for them to go where they want. The senseless driving is nothing more than a waste of money and fuel.

It is a classic confrontation: young persons (or the young-at-heart) wanting to do what they see as harmless behavior, while others, mostly older, want it stopped. It matters little that some of those older, more mature persons, who are now so opposed to it, were active participants when they were younger!

What is it about cruising, whether then or now, that attracts so many young people? *One way to understand this phenomenon is to see in it the sense of the significance that it brings.* For the few who spend so much time and effort to customize and modify their vehicles, showing them off gives a sense of significance that cannot be achieved only from the joy of doing the customizing and modifying. Rather, riding high above the others and seeing the stares and hearing the admiring comments from others make it all worthwhile.

The majority come downtown, however, just to be among friends. Seeing others and having others see you, even when there are few if any words exchanged, gives the young person a feeling of importance.

What is significance?
Significance, as we use it here, is a basic attitude or orientation toward oneself. It is not a fact that can be shown to be or not to be true, nor is it a feeling that can be identified. Significance is confirmed when others affirm the capabilities and accomplishments of a person. It is, on the other hand, damaged by lack of affirmation or communication; and when nothing is said verbally it is almost always interpreted as a negative response. Furthermore, an openly critical comment may shatter significance, resulting in depression that may last for days or weeks.

A family life education expert recently suggested that a *search for significance* lies behind the thinking and actions of youth in Western culture. He went on to say that in Western culture the need for significance is "more important than the need to survive. . . . We're the only creature that we know of that will voluntarily take our own life if we doubt its significance" ("Developing Capable Young

People—A Conversation with Stephen Glenn,"
Youthworker (Winter 1987), pp. 50-55.

The search is often very intense for teens who face severe doubts and questions about themselves. Many are not sure they like what is happening to their bodies even though they are growing quite normally. They have just adjusted to the last change when something else comes popping into their awareness. Think of the teenager for whom pimples—or worse yet, severe acne—seems to appear overnight.

Youth see many times each day society's image of the perfect body. Most youth have great trouble understanding that this image is achieved only in the photographer's studio. They feel woefully inadequate by comparison. It makes no difference that the advertising agency photographed many persons to find that image of perfection. The picture finally selected was taken from a precise, particular angle to give a very specific result.

Youth believe that they are totally unable to measure up to such images of perfection. This often leads them to question whether they are good enough for others. The result is a deep struggle with loneliness and depression because they believe there are so few people who really like them. These feelings are frequently compounded when adults communicate hostility because they cannot understand adolescent likes and dislikes, actions and attitudes.

Examples of significance search
The experiences of the following three typical teenagers help us understand better this search for significance.

Tom was fifteen years old when he volunteered to serve on a committee at church. The committee's task was to help the congregation evaluate its ministry and set goals for the future. The congregation had asked the youth group to select a person for this committee. Tom volunteered and that settled the matter very quickly. No one else was interested.

As time passed, Tom became less and less interested in attending the meetings of the committee. He complained that the meetings were boring. "All I do is sit there for two hours and don't say anything. It would not make any difference if I didn't go," he said. He did not feel that he was significant to the committee or to the youth whom he was supposedly representing. Several committee members encouraged him to stay with it and tried to help him get involved in the discussions. Others assured him that simply by being there he was making a contribution; he was keeping them aware that youth are an important part of the congregation.

Why did Tom volunteer in the first place? He would likely say he was not sure. He might have had some genuine interest in the church and how it goes about setting goals. More likely, Tom's primary reason for volunteering grew out of his search for something that would make him feel important. He wanted something that would somehow tell him he was really significant to the other youth in the group. Perhaps it would make the other youth in the group take notice of him and he would feel more a part of the group.

The initial affirmation did feel good. It also felt pretty good when several adults in the congregation said something to him when the committee began its work. But the good feeling soon wore off. None of the youth ever asked anything about it. Participation did not bring the expected feeling of significance.

Rhonda struggled with the fact that no one would ask her out. She spent time with friends and had an occasional date. But as she saw it, her older sister was always dating while she sat at home waiting. She decided that it must be because her sister was so slim and attractive. Rhonda saw herself as ugly and fat, even though she was not at all overweight.

So Rhonda began a diet and in a short time lost ten pounds. But the guys still did not call. She determined to lose even more. Her feelings of insignificance became so powerful and her desire to lose weight so strong that she began to force herself to vomit after eating.

At the same time she began to exercise far beyond what was necessary to keep physically fit, thinking this would burn calories so she would lose weight even faster. No matter how thin she became, she was obsessed with the idea that she was too fat. She lost so much weight that parents and others who cared for her became deeply alarmed. Ultimately she was diagnosed as being bulimic and anorexic. Her search for significance nearly cost Rhonda her life.

Rob was a fellow who got involved in everything possible. He played football in the fall, basketball in the winter, and ran track in the spring. He also played softball for his church team in the summer. He took private lessons on the trumpet and played in the school symphonic and jazz bands. He volunteered to be youth group president and was president of his school's honor society. He was not satisfied unless his grades earned him a place on the principal's honor roll.

For a time his parents and others marveled at his initiative and praised him for his obvious successes. However, the affirmation seemed to create a thirst for more in Rob. When his parents and friends began to question his busy schedule and expressed concern over how little sleep he was getting and that this might result in serious illness, he became irritated and impatient.

Then one day a close friend complained that Rob never had time to have fun like they'd once had. His girlfriend expressed resentment that he had so little time for her. He also heard of several youth who were frustrated that many youth group details were falling through the cracks. A long talk with his mentor—an adult friend in church—helped him see that he did not need to be superhuman to confirm his value and worth as a person. But deep inside, Rob continued to struggle with questions of whether he was really that important to anyone.

What is the meaning of the search?

How do we understand this longing for significance? Why do so many youth appear to struggle so intensely for it, going from one thing to another, a few into rebellious or unlawful behavior, in their search for it? Where do those who seem to be carefree, content, and confident find their sense of significance? Why does one sibling in a family seem to have developed a sound foundation for a sense of significance, while another appears to struggle a great deal?

Tom, Rhonda, and Rob illustrate the experience of many young persons who deeply, sometimes desperately, want to feel that they are important and that their lives make some difference to someone. Their search is for some evidence that will confirm that they are truly significant to others and themselves.

Significance often has roots deep within one's being and is shaped by the many and varied experiences of childhood. A warm, caring, affirming family experience can be the beginning of a solid foundation for a good attitude toward oneself. Building on this foundation later, a smile from a friend, praise from a parent on a job completed satisfactorily, or a word of encouragement from a teacher can support a teenager's sense of significance.

Among peers, the teen often interprets signals from others negatively. Teens experience a very uncertain world; they constantly look for signals from others. A comment may trigger fear that one does not fit in or that one is different from everyone else. The foundation they may have built during childhood nearly crumbles. Few have developed the inner resources that finally are the only reliable basis on which to argue with those things that continually seem to confirm their lack of significance.

Significance cannot be given to another. It is rather an inner conviction that is based on what is believed about the self, as well as about the world in which one lives. If that inner conviction tends to deny significance, affirmations and expressions of love and care may seem hollow and have little meaning. They only create a thirst for more. If, on the other hand, that inner conviction says that one is significant, warmth and affirmation from others simply confirm what exists inside.

How do teens experience significance?
Parents play a major role. Open, clear communication leads to trust and confidence on the part of teens and parents and contributes greatly to building significance. Affirmation and approval also help. Too frequently parents come across as demanding perfection. They are quick to point out faults and slow to compliment or affirm. Some claim that they are slow to affirm because they do not want their daughter or son to think they have done well enough and therefore will stop trying. However, if the parent will not give the needed affirmation, the teen will find it elsewhere.

The group they are "in" is important. Youth will often give great amounts of energy to getting in and staying in— sometimes at the expense of relationships with others who are important to them. Some will commit themselves to working long hours to have money for cars, clothes, cosmetics, or expensive electronic equipment. Using alcohol or illegal drugs often begins in the attempt to get into a group. Doing these things frequently leads to neglecting school studies and extra-curricular activities or spending time with parents and siblings.

Some adolescents believe that they will feel significance if they can find someone less well off than themselves. The competition can be intense for grades, for the most stylish clothes, or for the best stereo or computer. Some teens will do almost anything to keep another "below" them. It is in the interest of many in our culture to promote these attitudes, especially those whose business it is to market their products or maintain political power and authority.

Some young persons have found significance through joining a religious cult. They are attracted to such a cult

27

typically because of the acceptance, warmth, and love they feel from the first contact. They will attend a meeting even though they have no idea what it is about because of the promise of a good time and a certain caring attitude they feel in the invitation itself. The warmth and love meet a deep need. It is also the hook that cannot be resisted. The cult members make the visitor feel important to the group. In return, the young person will do anything that is asked. Too often teens end up giving their lives and possessions to the cause of the group and to its leader.

Others give themselves to the existing cultural system. They embrace its values, norms, and assumptions. In Western culture this often involves intense competition. Youth will pour great energy into their studies in order to get the best grades and gain admission to the most prestigious university. Their goal is a high-paying job, a house in an exclusive neighborhood, two expensive cars in their garage, and an annual trip to another part of the world. This is the "good life" and will surely provide great significance, even though it may be in the far distant future.

We see this approach in the experience of the rich young ruler as he met Jesus on the road (Mark 10). Here was a young man who, we might surmise, had been a serious student of what was considered most important in his day. He knew all the commandments. He went beyond intellectual knowledge to practice them conscientiously and had done so since the time of his youth.

While this rich young ruler was at the top academically, he also appeared to be financially secure. We are not told how he became so wealthy, but we sense that he could afford whatever he wanted. But neither his brains nor his money provided the sense of significance he desired. They were, however, too great a sacrifice when Jesus told him that these very things stood in the way of finding significance.

Some young persons make big commitments, overestimating the amount of significance they will get from it. They make the commitment more out of what they will get out of the experience than what they can contribute. Tom, whose story appeared earlier, is an example. When this happens, the feeling of insignificance grows even stronger and the youth will look for the first way to get out of the commitment.

Or, like Rhonda and Rob, it may lead to commitment to ideals or getting involved far beyond what is good for their physical, emotional, mental, and spiritual well-being. An increasing number feel like such a dismal failure that they decide it is no longer worth the effort. Attempts at suicide are a desperate call for attention to the inner struggle. Sadly, too many youth succeed.

The church's role

Feeling significant is as difficult for a young person who is a part of the church as for those who are not. This is true, in spite of the claim that youth in the church should have the best foundation for significance. Why do youth in the church struggle as much as others?

Adults in the church, just as adults in society in general, struggle to understand the younger set. In many congregations there are few close relationships between youth and adults, and in some congregations there is even a feeling of hostility. Some congregations are facing the fact that many of those who were born and reared in the church are dropping out in large numbers. Such circumstances hardly provide an attractive place to youth who have never been part of the church.

The church is only one of many voices within the culture that claims to be the best basis for significance. The many other voices that youth hear many times daily come to them with more slickness and pizzazz than many of us can even imagine! They are backed by an incredible investment of financial and creative resources. The church will never have similar resources available to it. Furthermore, one can find in the church skepticism, negative attitudes, and even hostility toward youth which make them feel unacceptable and insignificant.

The foundation for building significance

This chapter has focused mostly on those youth who struggle to find significance. Happily, we can point to some youth who are constructing a foundation on which true significance is built. These youth are characterized by a number of distinctive qualities.

Most importantly, these young persons have a basic understanding of who they are and a basic acceptance of themselves as they are—as unique, special individuals. They express a sense of confidence and trust, of peace and contentment. They recognize that they have much to learn and are eager to grow. They are open to the thoughts and ideas of others, but others do not control them. In short, they are free to be themselves.

Such young persons are characterized by a sense of purpose that grows out of appropriate goals they have set for themselves. It is a purpose that keeps in view both their own well-being and the well-being of others. Ironically, they are not really searching for significance. But, it comes as a gift! It is as Jesus said, "Those who find their life will lose it, and those who lose their life for my sake will find it" (Matthew 10:39).

The freedom and sense of purpose grow out of relationships rather than in what one does or says. They are found most fully in a relationship with Jesus Christ; they draw energy from the bond. The relationship gives a person true freedom. It is one in which one can know and feel forgiveness when there is failure. From it, one can respond in loving service to others who may be less fortunate, poor, or oppressed. It is a response that may even lead to suffering or death just as it did for Jesus.

Individuals with the qualities that we have just outlined have a high degree of maturity. Some would protest that few if any youth have such qualities. Nevertheless, we can see these qualities emerging in some teens. We see them in the young person who is able to resist the need to always dress in the latest fashions. We see them also in the teens who have committed themselves to give a tithe of all they earn to the church or the one who actively participates in the life of the congregation. It is seen in those youth who commit themselves to be and become unique expressions of God's love in the world.

Biblical examples
We also see these qualities modeled in various biblical persons.

John the Baptist committed himself to preparing others for the coming of another who would be the true source of significance. His commitment led to imprisonment and ultimately, to death.

Mary was one whose commitment to a cause beyond herself gave her a sense of appropriate priorities as she took time to learn from the Master Teacher even when her sister asked that she help prepare the meal.

Paul, born Saul, caught a vision of the better way on the road to Damascus, which led to spreading the gospel to the Gentile world.

Jesus Christ is the supreme illustration of one who gave his life for others. His ministry to others provided the way out of poverty, oppression, hopelessness, and despair as he ministered to the whole person. He was not concerned with finding significance for himself, but in the end, his life and ministry changed the course of the whole world.

Can the church reach out to youth, affirm them as valued persons, and help them construct a firm foundation on which they can base significance? It must! If it desires to be a church that is truly responsive to the needs of youth, it has no alternative. To do so requires, first of all, that it understand the other voices that call to youth. We will in the next chapter reflect briefly on the content of their message and how it is communicated. The church must also recognize that it is one of those voices and therefore, must continually think very carefully how it reaches out to and communicates with its youth.

Chapter 4: INFLUENCERS AND PERSUADERS: promising significance

Influencers and persuaders know that youth feel significant when they are affirmed. They also know that adolescence is a time of trying many different things.

The time and money that young persons spend shopping, trying on clothes to find the perfect outfit for the next day, standing in front of the mirror, worrying about friendships, and a host of other activities are largely an investment in finding significance. Many persons, groups, and institutions in Western culture have caught on to this phenomenon. These are the influencers and persuaders. All promise that their idea, product, or service will surely lead to significance. Who are these influencers and persuaders who are targeting the teen world with their messages?

Entertainers
Perhaps those who present their case most strongly to youth are those who entertain them day after day. Their music often presents a fantasy world which claims that significance can be found quickly and easily with little or no effort. Romantic love is presented as the most important thing in all of life. It is presented in terms of physical sexuality, often through cheap romance and one-night sexual encounters. Or, listeners are invited to drown their loneliness and depression in drugs and alcohol.

Motion pictures and television entertainers present a dream world that scarcely resembles reality. Conflict is resolved too easily with guns and violence or by lying or telling half-truths. Those who are different are frequently made to look stupid or funny. Significance is found in being the toughest, most deceptive, and domineering. It is found in winning at all costs.

The world of sports in particular emphasizes significance through winning. Peers and the entire community become impatient and critical with their school's athletes when they are having a losing season. Success comes only in winning, not in participation and playing to the best of one's abilities. This is compounded at the professional level where winning has become connected with huge salaries and expectations of bringing that winning edge that one person alone can only rarely bring to the team. Yet these sports figures as entertainers suggest a false hope to millions of youth who think they might find significance through similar means.

Entertainers do play an important role in our society. They can help people express their deepest feelings through music or the arts. In a fast-paced society, they can help us slow down, be reflective, and even help us be critical of other elements in the culture. Sometimes they help us laugh at ourselves. Some entertainers have brought and are bringing into their messages an appeal that confronts injustice, oppression, and poverty.

Sadly, however, most seem to be in the field only for the money, accumulating as much as they possibly can, regardless of their message and how it affects or influences their listeners and fans.

Buyers and sellers

The entertainment industry survives on the basis of selling its products—concerts and games, compact discs, tapes, movies, and videos. But it also depends on its ability to sell the products of another group which has a great impact on teens. This group makes its money through its ability to persuade others to buy its goods and services. They are often able to persuade youth of "needs" that really do not exist. These are the buyers and sellers.

The buyers and sellers appeal to youth primarily through advertisements. Advertisers spend a lot of time and money on each advertisement, whether in television commercials or in magazines or newspapers. The message to the viewer or reader is that the product advertised is much better than any other. Wearing a certain brand of clothing, using this toothpaste or that shampoo and conditioner, or owning a certain piece or brand of electronic equipment will bring greater happiness and contentment than could ever happen without it. Sometimes all that is needed is to convince one or two youths, and before long, everyone in the whole school is convinced.

Ironically, when one is finally won over, the same brand suddenly appears "new and improved" or the styles change. The task of convincing begins all over. Teens, with their strong need for significance, are particularly vulnerable—especially when a favorite singer or actress or sports personality is the one telling them that a product must be purchased.

As with the entertainers, we can acknowledge the helpful and necessary role that many buyers and sellers play in our society. Through the initiative and creativity of some, products are made available that reduce the stress of life and make it better for many persons. Many also contribute a great deal to support worthwhile projects and programs.

But too often, the buyers and sellers make huge profits regardless of the half-truths that are designed to create desires for things that persons simply do not need.

Politicians
Another group of influencers and persuaders invites teens to find their significance through the political system. These persons claim, first of all, that one political or economic system is better than any other. Furthermore, they claim their particular party's view of that system is better

than another. In Western society politicians continually praise the democratic system and denounce communism and socialism as the reason for the world's sorry state.

It is the business of the politician to convince people that a particular way of seeing the world is best, both for the individual and for the entire nation. Their message to teens is often that each one deserves to have wants and desires fulfilled regardless of what it will do to others in the neighborhood or in other parts of the world.

Thus the message of the politician has to do with power. This is particularly obvious during election times when the various parties—Liberals, Conservatives, Republicans, Democrats—try to persuade the voters to elect their candidates. Incredible promises and impressive commitments, often forgotten soon after the election, are made to convince the voter. Groups with special interests give large sums of money to certain candidates who will represent their particular interest. The promise that their power and influence will insure safety, freedom, and the best environment to pursue the good life appeals to teens in their insecurities.

Once again, the appropriate role of the politicians must be noted. Sensitive persons who will make laws that provide for the good of all are needed to serve in government. Such public servants attempt to keep in perspective the needs of those in our own nation and throughout the world. Unfortunately, far too many politicians lose sight of the good of all and only protect their own narrow interests and the interests of those who helped them get elected.

The Military
Still another group of influencers and persuaders are those who are involved in the development of huge military organizations that make more and more powerful weapons. In many countries this group has become so powerful that they virtually control the governmental decisions and political processes. They operate by keeping the general public in constant fear of the possibility of an attack from an

enemy force. They claim the need for greater and more powerful weapons to keep up with those that other superpowers have. Those countries not claiming superpower status are forced to declare their allegiance to one side or the other as allies.

The military must have teens to staff their machine. Through slick advertisements promising education, adventure, and training that will lead to a high-paying job after their military duty is completed, they persuade many teens to commit a substantial portion of their lives to the cause of the military. Once they are "hooked," these young recruits are programmed to believe that it is right and good to kill other human beings if they can be identified as enemies. Significance, they say, comes in protecting one's country, even if it means killing another human person.

Schools

All of the influencers and persuaders noted above must find ways to communicate to young persons. They hope that teens will consume their products or agree with them now and in the future as well. The entertainers must continually increase the numbers who will purchase their products and the products of those who sponsor them. The politician influencers want to increase the number who will keep them in power. They also want young persons who will give themselves not only to their view of life but also to staffing the military machine.

In a word, competition is at the heart of the message of all the influencers and persuaders. The unwritten expectation is to get to the "top." The public school is often seen as the vehicle to communicate this message. William Meyers, in his book *Theological Themes of Youth Ministry* (New York: Pilgrim Press, 1987, p. 6), says that competition is at the very heart of the public school system. He says:

> Designed with competition in mind, the high school is tied to its culture. Competition is a cultural value undergirded by complementary values like position,

material acquisition, and power. These values are what finally determine the high school's educational form . . . which allow[s] only a select few to reach the top. The end goal of education is articulated as *success*. Survive the competition and you will succeed. You will receive the "A," the "best athlete," or "most popular" award. School is to be understood as a mirror of real life: beat the other person or get beaten yourself. Survive. Compete.

In a real sense, the school is in and of itself, one of the influencers and persuaders. Its primary task is to educate the nation's youth. But it does so from a particular perspective which includes the preservation of the culture's most important values and beliefs. Getting ahead or to the top, through competition and success at any cost, is at the heart of the way the school approaches its task.

The school is also the place where the messages of the other influencers and persuaders get to youth. The politicians hold the purse strings of the school system. This assures that the school will not stray far from the values and beliefs the culture holds most dear. Military recruiters are also given free access to students in all-school assemblies.

Some churches have responded by establishing private schools which are operated by their own board of directors and financed fully by private funds. In these schools students can become critical of the predominant culture's values from the perspective of faith. Such criticism includes affirming those values that are not in conflict with their faith perspective. It also helps youth find alternative ways of thinking where there is conflict. Many such private schools, however, have not taken seriously their role as critics of the culture. They sometimes more strongly support the culture's values than is the case even in the public school.

Youth—oppressed and manipulated

The influencers and persuaders know that many teens are

not skilled in, nor have they had much help in, making decisions. They also know that youth feel significant when they are affirmed. They know that adolescence is a time of trying many different things, especially those things modeled by persons they admire most. Many sincerely believe that their answers are the best. But others know better. They see adolescents as a group that can be taken advantage of to further their own goals. Michael Warren, a leading Catholic educator and youth ministry writer, in his book *Youth and the Future of the Church* (New York: Seabury Press, 1982), says:

> Young people in our society are among the most oppressed and manipulated segments of the population. They are oppressed because they are voiceless and therefore powerless; they are manipulated because they are unaware of the structures and systems that control their lives. These structures and systems include the educational structures, the economic structures, especially the structures for marketing and advertising; the entertainment industry, especially its subset, the music industry; the religious structures; and the political structures, especially as they effect the potential militarization of our young men and young women.

If, as Warren says, youth today are oppressed and manipulated, we must ask why they allow themselves to be oppressed and manipulated like this. Is it a case of ignorance, of not knowing what is really taking place? Perhaps, but we must also acknowledge that the message of the influencers and persuaders comes to them in a way that touches their most basic needs and insecurities.

The message of the entertainer, the politician, the military, and the buyer and seller comes to them softly but powerfully. Rarely do they openly criticize how things are. In their messages they convey a sense of how important the young person is. The young person gets the underlying message that says, "You can be significant!"

While doing this they also present an ideal—the glamorous, perfect woman and the handsome, secure gentleman—that leaves the young person feeling terribly inadequate. Then they say, just as strongly, "*You* can be our ideal, more 'ok,' liked more and appreciated—if you will just do what we tell you and follow our way!" This message is strong and forceful yet at the same time subtle and controlled, communicated with great sensitivity to its hearers. Because of this it is difficult to resist, especially for those who do not have the experience that helps them hear or understand the meanings behind what is communicated on the surface.

The church as influencer and persuader

The church also comes to youth with a message that claims to be the basis for significance. It is a message similar in certain respects to the message of the entertainers, the politicians, the military, and the buyers and sellers.

The church wants to communicate to the youth that they are loved, valued and affirmed. The church values youth, not because of their potential as purchasers of goods and services which are produced, but rather because they are creations of a loving and caring God. In contrast to the other influencers and persuaders, the church loves its young persons because they are persons who are loved and valued first of all by God. They matter, not because they can help maintain power like the politician, but rather because their presence, vitality, and enthusiasm are gifts to the congregation.

The church invites youth, without pressure, to accept its way of life. We can find some similarities in the basic message of the church and all the other influencers and persuaders. But the way it communicates that message must be different in every respect. The invitation the church extends is in contrast to the subtle and controlling approach of many entertainers, buyers and sellers, and politicians. This method, of course, leaves the church open to the possibility of its youth rejecting its message. It must therefore be ready to suffer pain when this happens.

The church will encourage young people to grow and develop at their own pace. It will take very seriously the uniqueness of each one and encourage them to make commitments along the way in their own time. This does not mean that the church will be careless in communicating its message. It will use every means available to share it with them but will always leave them free to respond as they will.

The message of the church will result in a lasting, meaningful significance because its foundations are built from within. The message of the other influencers and persuaders produces short-term satisfaction and leads to a fleeting sense of significance.

The message of the church is that significance comes in finding wholeness as a person through a relationship with Jesus Christ and in extending that wholeness to others. Significance is not gained in being self-centered, in accumulating great wealth and material possessions, or in gathering power to oneself. It is found in being a person of peace, justice and reconciliation, helping others become whole. Thus it frees others from oppression and suffering.

To be the bearer of this message is to express God's love. Lasting, meaningful significance comes, as these ideas suggest, in being an expression of God's love in the world. Congregational youth ministry is helping young persons *be and become expressions of God's love in their world.*

PART II: Congregation

Our primary task in this book is the development of a blueprint for youth ministry in the congregation which has as its ultimate goal an even more important construction project. This is the building of the lives of youth. The congregation must not assume, however, that it can or should build the lives of its young persons. Rather, it provides the environment and support system that enable youth to build their own lives. It is a building project in which the church along with many persons, groups, and institutions—influencers and persuaders—have great interest.

The church is one among various influencers and persuaders in our society to respond to youth in their search for significance. How it does this is extremely important if it is to be truly helpful in satisfying youth's deep longing. Effective youth ministry will enable and help youth to be and become expressions of God's love in the world. In so doing youth will find the only lasting significance.

The temptation is to move immediately to thinking about a youth ministry program to carry out this youth ministry vision. However, before developing a specific program, it is crucial that congregations seriously consider the environment in which such a ministry can be carried out. Without doing this, a youth ministry program can be as manipulative and oppressive as the message of any other influencer and persuader.

To be a place where youth can truly find significance as an expression of God's love in the world, congregations must see themselves as a community of faith, and must carefully develop biblically-based beliefs about youth and faith. The following chapters address these two important areas.

Chapter 5: THE COMMUNITY OF FAITH: enabling Christ-centered identities

To be a place where youth can truly find significance as an expression of God's love in the world, congregations must carefully develop biblically-based beliefs about youth and faith.

The church—a context in which to build

Does the church have anything to offer teenagers who are concerned by many decisions which are typically made on the basis of what will bring significance? Can the church be a helpful resource to adolescents as they shape and develop their identity?

The answer to both of these questions must be a clear and firm yes. Unfortunately, however, many congregations have not been helpful to their young people. These congregations have taken their cues from the entertainers, the buyers and sellers, and the politicians, often borrowing their tactics to "win" teens to their way of life. They try to give youth the answers without helping them develop their own convictions. These congregations tend to see the adolescent years as a stage that must be endured. It is sad that this view of youth has resulted in many of them dropping out of church as teens or later as young adults.

Congregations who are interested in the total welfare of youth will, rather, provide a context in which youth can authentically build their own lives. Michael Warren is correct when he says,

> It is the nature of young people to have to discover their
> own word of faith. The flower of faith cannot be trans-
> planted because it would then be one person's flower of
> faith, growing in another person's soil. The flower of
> faith has to grow from seed in each person's special
> soil and grow as one's own flower ("Can Liturgy Speak
> to Young People?" *Readings and Resources in Youth
> Ministry*, Michael Warren, ed. Winona, Minnesota: St.
> Mary's Press, 1987, p. 33).

Congregations that help youth, as Warren suggests, to
grow their own special "flowers of faith" will walk with
youth in ways that help them develop biblically-based values and beliefs. They will see the teen years as critically
important years in shaping identity—forming the heart—
the foundation for being and becoming unique expressions of God's love in the world. Congregations that do this
will see themselves as a *community of faith.*

A congregation that understands itself as a community
of faith asks more about about the process of how youth
make decisions than in the end result, although it is deeply
interested in the decisions they make. It asks how it can
assist as their identities take shape, helping them grow
more and more to be like Christ.

A brief look back
Most congregations would claim to think of themselves in
this way. Yet a brief examination of youth ministry in my
denomination, the Mennonite Church, during the past several decades, suggests that our actions have not kept up
with what we have claimed. Other denominations have
reported similar experiences.

An older man, perhaps in his seventies, telephoned my
office to vent some anger. He was responding to an article I
had written on the history of organized youth group activities in the Mennonite Church. In the late 1940s, he said,
his ministers announced that the next Sunday there would

be a new youth fellowship. The current youth activity, known as a *literary society*, would be ended.

"They never even asked us whether we wanted it or not," he said in obvious anger. He went on to explain that he had been a leader in his literary society. After nearly four decades he was still angry that this had been taken from him, even though he could now admit that the new youth fellowship has been good for the church.

The late 1940s reflect a time of renewed interest in ministry with youth. That decade saw the development of highly structured denominational, district, and congregational youth group programs. Specific activities were suggested for the congregation and new materials were written to help make it happen.

The reasons for this new development are not entirely clear. It may have been the realization that large numbers of young persons would soon be coming on the scene as a result of the baby boom following World War II. Another concern described in various documents from that time was that youth were not included nor were they participating in the life of the congregation. What was taking place was outside of the congregation with little shaping by and influence from congregational leaders. Leaders hoped that this new structure would bring youth more closely into the total program of the congregation.

The *youth group*, as the new youth fellowship came to be called, for many years proved to be a very useful setting for supporting and nurturing youth. Youth grew spiritually as they discussed issues and concerns, developed leadership skills, and served persons in need. Many parents today recall that the youth group was the only acceptable place for them to socialize and develop friendships.

In the late 1980s, many of the churchwide structures have been phased out as have those in many district conferences. Even though many congregations continue an effective youth group program, an increasing number are questioning whether the church continues to be effective in reaching their youth.

What is happening now?

Other sources of entertainment compete with youth group. Concerts, movies, cruising, and especially television and the home video often seem more exciting than youth group. Young persons will no longer tolerate a boring program, because they can choose from so many other activities. This has placed additional pressure on the adult sponsors or youth pastor to make the youth program as good as these other exciting events. When this happens, congregations have trouble finding sponsors. Or a youth pastor, if one has been employed, stays only a brief time.

The youth group no longer enjoys the high priority it once did. This is true for both youth and their parents, especially when it comes to attending and participating regularly. Parents, however, still expect a high quality program . . . in case their son or daughter might decide to attend. We have already noted that many parents today permit their youth to be involved in a much wider variety of activities than was once the case. This has had great impact on how the youth group has functioned.

Adult leaders are taking greater responsibility in maintaining a quality program. As youth give the activities of the group lower priority, leaders step in to meet the continuing high expectations of parents and other adults. Some congregations turn to an employed youth pastor to pick up the responsibility and make the youth group a good experience. The youth group becomes and continues to be centered in the adult leaders.

In many congregations the youth program is viewed as "their program" rather than "our program." This is perhaps the first sign of serious trouble in youth ministry. Many times only a few members of the congregation are personally involved in it. There are few meaningful relationships between youth and adults. Yet the congregation continues to have high expectations of the youth program.

The youth group becomes a parallel congregation separate from the adult congregation. The high expectations of the congregation and the low personal involvement with the youth often result in adults being quick to criticize what is or is not happening. The adult sponsors find themselves in the uncomfortable position of being the bridge between the two groups.

Fewer and fewer adults are interested in serving as youth group sponsors. Nor will the circumstances attract and invite youth to identify with and develop loyalty to the church. We find ourselves in a situation where we once more need new understandings and approaches that will invite and welcome youth into the congregation as a vital part of its life.

The congregation as a community of faith

The time has come to again ask how youth can be *a part of*, not *apart from*, the congregation. If we can help youth see the congregation as a resource for their decision making, they will find it a place that leads to true significance. The congregation will then be in a position to help them build a Christ-centered identity. The congregation will see youth ministry as a ministry of the whole church. It will not be a ministry only of the youth pastor or youth sponsors. This calls for congregations to see themselves as a *community of faith.*

A variety of images has been used to describe the church. Some see it as a place where sick people come—a hospital—to be healed from the pain and suffering of life. Others see it as a service station, a place to come once a week to get pumped up and refueled to go back into the "real world" of work or school or home during the week. Still others see it primarily as a place where certain rituals and ceremonies are carried out in an appropriate manner which keeps the participants in God's favor no matter how the rest of life is lived.

Seeing the congregation as a community of faith means that *every participant is seen as crucial to its existence.* Every participant is of great value and worth as a person within the community. The congregation is an integral part of life. It is a point of reference which helps make sense out of what is happening in one's world. In light of the other noisy influencers and persuaders, it helps keep in clear perspective the quieter sources of significance that come from being a unique expression of God's love in the world.

We have already noted that the church is an influencer and persuader and carries similar concern for youth as all other influencers and persuaders. However, as a community of faith its message is centered in Jesus Christ, God's only son. The way it communicates that message is totally different from the way the influencers and persuaders communicate.

The message

Through God's Word, the Bible, we learn that Jesus was sent into the world in human form as a new expression of God's desire to be in relationship with us and to provide a way to make that relationship possible. God created the world and all that is in it. The most special part of that creation was the human person, made for the purpose of being in relationship with God. But the relationship was broken. Even so, God kept reaching out in love, seeking to reestablish communication. The ultimate invitation came in Jesus Christ. Through Jesus Christ the way for relationship with God was opened anew.

The message of Jesus threatened the religious structures of the day. It destroyed the established pattern that said that persons could only relate to God through the religious leaders and by doing what they said. It threatened the economic and political structures which were deeply connected with the religious structures. No longer did people need to purchase expensive items for their religious rituals, They could have their own personal relationship with God!

The message also threatened the social structures which rigidly kept certain individuals and groups in submission to the authorities. Women were honored by Jesus, as were all who were poor and oppressed. Those who were avoided and condemned because they were ill or deformed were healed. The threat was so great that those in power decided they must kill Jesus. In executing Jesus as a common criminal, they thought they could silence this person who upset everything.

The message does not end in death, however, but in a risen Christ who lives, making possible a relationship with God through a commitment to Jesus Christ. Within the community of faith such a relationship can be planted and nurtured. Through the support and discipline of a relationship within the community, life can be lived as modeled by Jesus himself in loving service to others.

This message strongly counters the messages of the entertainer, the politician, and the other influencers, who do everything possible to convince us that self-centeredness and financial security is the source of significance. It is a message that says to youth that significance is found in being for others, not in competitive attitudes or activities designed to prove one is better or of higher status.

As a community of faith, the church values and cherishes every participant, including each child, young person, and adult. It sees gifts in each participant who can therefore "gift" the community with a special contribution. It also values the potential in each person for growth toward Christlikeness and provides opportunity and challenge to ongoing growth.

This approach is based on deep interest and love for each person. It provides the space and freedom to grow and develop at an individual pace and offers the deepest level of care and support. At the same time, it never neglects opportunities to encourage and challenge each participant to grow in all areas of life. It will educate to encourage growth toward wholeness. It will also provide opportunities for each young person to discover and develop their giftedness and find ways where those gifts can be used in service to others both within the community of faith and outside.

In a community of faith, persons are not seen as objects

to be acted upon, but rather as persons who are actively involved. They are shaping their own life which will in turn shape the life of the community. Therefore, it is a context for working seriously at their decisions out of their commitment to Jesus as Lord and Savior. The community respects the freedom that young persons need in their experimenting, but one which will walk closely with them as they do this.

A community of faith will see its youth as a vital, important part of the congregation. It will minister to each young person, inviting them to grow in becoming unique expressions of God's love in the world. It also sees youth as having the ability to minister to each other as well as to persons in other generations. The entire congregation is involved in ministry to and with youth, not just a few designated leaders. It uses many settings for this ministry, not just the youth group.

William Meyers, in his book *Theological Themes of Youth Ministry* (New York: Pilgrim Press, 1987, pp. 11-12), summarizes this community of faith in this way:

I have long suggested that ministry *with* youth should be an operating metaphor for youth ministry. Here the community asks member youth to serve. Not by themselves, but as part of the community. So a high school junior and a senior might help a lay person and the pastor teach a confirmation group. Such service, such ministry makes excellent sense. Some of this service is occasional, some is regularized, but here are many hints as to the presence of this Diakonia service. Do youth serve on official boards? Do they pledge? Are they occasional lay readers on Sunday? If there is a youth committee, are half its members youth? Do older youth care for younger youth in the community? Does the church community reach, via its youth, outside the church? Whatever the form, such all-hands-involved service embodies Diakonia ministry. In this community all are called to serve, including youth.

Mitch, a high school senior, had this to say in church the day he graduated: "Soon I'll be leaving this place, but not really. You will go with me. You treated me like a real person. I argued with you, prayed with you, and even preached with you. You helped me when I was hurting, and I believe I helped you when I could see your hurt. I was a teacher for the confirmation program and a regular participant in worship. Those were the sharing places that helped me grow."

Chapter 6: CONGREGATIONAL YOUTH MINISTRY: foundational beliefs

If we truly believe that youth are created to live in the image of God . . . we will see them as persons who are responsible for "working out their own salvation" in growing awareness that it is Christ who is working within.

In the community of faith, our reasons for becoming involved in youth ministry grow out of deep interest in and love for young persons. Our deepest longing is that their identities be Christ-centered and that they come to discover significance as expressions of God's love in the world.

Approaching youth ministry in this way requires that we examine our basic beliefs about children and youth. Our theology of youth ministry contains those beliefs about God and God's concern for each young person. In this chapter we cannot set out a complete theology of youth ministry. However, three beliefs form the foundation for our youth ministry rebuilding project:

1. *God is Creator*
2. *God through Christ provides the way of salvation*
3. *God continues to be present in the Holy Spirit*

God is Creator

The beginning point of a theology of youth ministry is to recognize and affirm that God created the whole world and everything in it. The Genesis Creation accounts help us know a God who is deeply involved in the affairs of the world and has been so since the very beginning. God's creation was nothing short of a labor of love and we, the human race, are the special focus of God's love.

Furthermore, God's very self was invested in each one created. Genesis 1:26 affirms the fact that the human person was created in the image of God. Many writers have attempted to explain this concept. I have found it meaningful to reflect on the investment that loving parents make in their children as a way to get a glimpse of what it means.

Many parents invest great amounts of love and care in each of their children. They do this as they provide shelter, food, clothing, and other necessities. They assist in their education and offer support when the going is difficult. Parents encourage their children to pursue what is right and good.

Much of this suggests financial investment. More important, however, is the commitment of time, energy, and emotion. Parents are thrilled when a daughter or son makes choices that show growth in being all that God intended. But the pain and suffering can be equally great when parents see a son or daughter making choices that suggest movement away from or rejection of Christian values.

Many of us know how much parents invest in each of their children. This in a small way helps us understand how much God invested in creating each one of us. Something of God's own self has been planted within every person. God wants to see this plant take root and grow to be an expression of the divine creation love.

Implications
That we have been created by God in God's image has a number of very important implications for ministry with youth.

First of all, God's love has never been withdrawn in spite of our frequent turning away. It is a love that reaches out to every person—every child, every *young person*, every adult. This is especially important for those who commit themselves to work with youth. Very often youth's frantic search for significance makes it a struggle to see the potential that God placed in each one.

But God loves them and that is reason enough for us to reach out in love to them. Youth are worthy of our love. This is not because of what they can do for us, as the other influencers and persuaders think. No, we love them regardless of how unattractive they may be because God has loved them first!

This makes the motivation for, and importance of, youth ministry perfectly clear. Every young person, within the church and outside, is worth our time and energy. We must therefore think carefully about how we can help them grow and build their lives through the programs that we develop and carry out in the congregation.

We noted earlier that many congregations have not taken this responsibility seriously. Far too many children born into the church have lost interest in the church and as youth and young adults leave and never return.

Secondly, a loving God would never create one person of greater value than another. This certainty gives us the most helpful response to one of youth's deepest struggles. They are constantly encouraged to compare themselves to others. Furthermore, the message that comes to them always implies that others are just a little better off because they are the center of attention, have more things, or are more talented. Advertisers suggest that by a purchase or two they can become like everyone else.

In God's love, every person is created of equal worth and value. This does not mean that all humans are alike. God created each person as a unique individual. There are no carbon copies and no clones.

Difference is nothing more or less than uniqueness. *It does not suggest greater value or worth.* It is difficult for many teens to understand that differences in persons create a wonder and delight. To loving parents and youth leaders each is an artwork of infinitely greater beauty than any by Rembrandt or Michelangelo! How boring it would be without the differences and the uniquenesses found in the human race. Young people are a special part of that creation. Because God is their creator they can know that they have as much value and worth as anyone else, regardless of their looks, possessions, or status. This is an extremely important point for youth to understand. It is often, however, so hard for them to believe.

Thirdly, being created in God's image gives focus to our efforts in helping youth develop their unique identity. In youth ministry our deepest desire is that young persons will allow the seed of God's image to grow as their identity takes shape.

Again, the investment that loving parents make in their children helps us understand this. The return on this investment is seeing something of themselves in their children. Parents see the return in the qualities of life that emerge, the values that take shape, and most visibly, in the choices that grow out of these qualities of life and values.

In a similar way, as we work with youth, we want them to learn of the God who created them. As a result, we want them to reflect the image of their heavenly parent. Indeed, it is a growing process toward living in the image of God so that God's love is visible to others around them. The image of God is, therefore, central to the development of each young person's identity. Furthermore, it provides the only lasting source of significance.

It must be clear that as humans we will never fully live in that image. To suggest that God has made an immense investment in creating the human person is not to suggest that we can ever become God. We can, however, seek to help youth understand God's intention in creation as the basis for forming their identity in God's image and living in that image. Then in the face of the many other voices competing for their attention, they will have a firm foundation upon which to base their response.

God through Christ provides a way of salvation

We are not left to ourselves to figure out what it means to live in the image of God. God made that clear by sending Jesus Christ into the world. In Jesus we see God's intention in creation most fully. We also can see what it means to live in God's image. Jesus, as the supreme expression of God's love, calls persons to wholeness, to justice, to peace, and to right relationships.

Throughout the Scriptures, especially in the Gospels, we see God's concern for the poor and oppressed. Jesus brought healing to the sick and wholeness to those who were broken. He called persons to live in right relationships with others. Jesus confronted those who abused their positions of power and challenged them to do justice. He reached out with respect to those who were cast off in society. In doing this he upset the status quo so much that he was ultimately executed on a cross.

The example of Jesus provides a clear model for carrying out the intention of God in creation. Our vocation as Christians is to live in that image as persons of justice, love, and peace. This is a high calling!

To envision a world where love, justice, and peace are lived requires an act of the imagination. Reality keeps barging in to show us how far from this ideal our world is. We see poverty, oppression, injustice, and hatred all around us. And to complete the grim picture, we live under a darkening cloud of nuclear madness that could bring an end to life on this planet as we know it.

But God calls us to imagine a world of wholeness, of peace, and of reconciliation between enemies. The so-called reality says this is not possible. Our commitment to live as Jesus did—imaging God—will not let us give in to that so-called reality but will give us the courage and strength to dream the impossible!

Jesus did not only show what it means to live in God's image; God, through Christ, went far beyond that to extend to us forgiveness for sin. One way that sin has been defined is "missing the mark." We said earlier that Jesus made

God's intention in creation clear—to live in justice, reconciliation, and peace. Too frequently we fail miserably to live up to this high calling of God in Christ Jesus. Sometimes we do so unintentionally, but too often we sin deliberately, being fully aware of our actions.

We sin when we do not accept the fact of God's creation work and reject God's love, choosing instead to rely on the other influencers and persuaders to confirm our significance. We sin when we put others down in an effort to bolster our feeling of being valued. We sin when we refuse to develop and use our gifts in expressing God's love to others. Sin is when we know what is right and fail to do it.

God graciously provides forgiveness for our sinful ways through Jesus' death on the cross and resurrection. We need only respond in faith to God's gracious act, confess our sin, and commit ourselves to follow Jesus.

Jesus is the one who shows how we can truly live as expressions of God's love in the world. He taught and demonstrated that meaningful life is found in loving God and loving our neighbor. The foundation for significance comes through recognizing ourselves as creations of God. We can respond by allowing God to shape and form our image after God's own, through which we express God's love to others.

Implications
That God sent Jesus into the world to show us what it means to live in God's image and as the means of salvation has several implications for our ministry with youth.

First of all, we can present the vision of God's intention for all creation—to live as Jesus taught and lived. The teen years are often a time of high idealism. Young persons can reach beyond themselves to try things that older, more experienced adults think is impossible. This gives us an excellent opportunity to challenge and catch their imagination.

Secondly, we can help youth understand and deal with sin in their lives. Teenagers often sense keenly what is right or wrong but feel powerless to do anything about it on their own. Sin is more fully understood in relationship to specific, concrete acts than it is in being lost or in being sinful by nature. They feel deeply the tension between knowing what is right and finding themselves incapable of doing it. They know that they often miss the mark of God's intention for their lives.

Consequently, youth often feel they are in a bind and they struggle to be free. Those who minister with youth can help them accept the forgiveness for sin that is offered through Christ. It is our privilege to invite them to a commitment to Christ as Savior and Lord.

Youth from different backgrounds
In inviting youth to accept salvation, we must be sensitive to the background of each youth.

Those from Christian families. For young people born into families that are part of the community of faith, it may be a recognition and affirmation of a commitment made as a child. They have been nurtured in this loving community to understand God's intention in creation. As young people they are encouraged to make a voluntary commitment to Jesus Christ that is much more clearly their own. Moving from the faith of a child to the more mature personal commitment may be accompanied by a period of questioning and doubt. The church recognizes this as a part of normal growth and development as the youth progresses in her or his faith journey.

Birth is the beginning of the salvation process for children in the community of faith. As infants they feel the warmth and loving care of parents and others surrounding them. This is a nurturing process that helps them deal with sin as they learn to recognize it. According to Marlin Jeschke, in his book *Believer's Baptism for Children of the Church* (Scottdale, Pa.: Herald Press, 1983, p. 143), " . . . to be privileged to grow up within the community of faith and own that faith when reaching the age of discretion is the more excellent way." Jeschke states further that it is an experience "of appropriation and ownership of the faith in which they have been brought up, even if that appropriation includes willing rejection of the non-Christian way, the renunciation of the devil and all his works" (pp. 142-43).

Those who have not experienced a Christian family. A community of faith will also find ways to reach out in mission to youth who have never experienced the loving care of parents or the influence of a community of faith. These youth may not know of the love of God. A congregation will also continually seek for ways to relate to those who have known such a loving God but have chosen to reject that call. It will recognize in these persons that the seed planted has not been nourished. Nevertheless it continues to remain ready for watering and nurturing, leading to growth if the young person will become open to God's work within, confessing the sin that separates them from God and responding in commitment to Christ.

Salvation — a process, unique for each person

Above all, in a community of faith, commitment to Christ will be a voluntary response to God's love and call. Leaders will never use force, neither will they manipulate young persons to get them to respond. Furthermore, as we walk with youth, we can recognize that it is God who is at work causing a growing awareness of sin and creating a desire for right relationships. It is also an awareness that through the grace of God, there is forgiveness when we do sin. God frequently communicates this awareness through the community of faith but also deals directly with individuals. In whatever way God chooses to work, it is a transforming work that allows the image of God to become increasingly visible as the young person grows in commitment to Christ.

Salvation, from this perspective, is a process unique for each young person. For some, who have been seen as an important part of the congregation from the time they were infants, its beginning will hardly be noticed. For others, like the Apostle Paul, it will be a jolting, surprising revelation that was never anticipated. Salvation may be a decision made out of intense struggle resulting in a dramatic, drastic change of life.

However it begins, it begins a lifelong transformation process of living more and more in the image of God. It is a gift of God freely given to those who claim it.

God continues to be present in the Holy Spirit

As Jesus left the disciples to ascend to be with God, he left the promise of the Holy Spirit to be God's continuing presence with them. The Holy Spirit would guide them into truth and would help them know the will of God from that time on. The Holy Spirit would be God's representative to those who believed after Christ was no longer present with them. More importantly, the Holy Spirit would empower them to carry on the work that Christ began in his ministry on earth.

Implications

The Holy Spirit was sent at Pentecost and continues to be present in those who commit themselves to Christ. This basic belief also has significant implications for ministry with youth.

First of all, helping youth come to know the presence of the Holy Spirit can be a great comfort in their times of loneliness. Many youth struggle a great deal, feeling that they are alone and have no friends. Often feeling that they are on the outside, assurance of the Holy Spirit as a friend and guide can help them through these tough times.

Secondly, young persons can be helped to see that the Holy Spirit empowers them to respond to the gift of salvation. This response can take a variety of forms. One form will be the discipline that an individual gives to her or his own formation process. Growth in living in the image of God, in being and becoming unique expressions of God's love in the world, does not just happen. Rather, it takes place in an ongoing way as one gives oneself to Jesus

Christ in a disciplined commitment to understand more fully God's intentions in the world. Through personal study, reflection, and commitment to and participation in the community of faith as it gathers for worship and discernment of God's will, the young person can grow to live more and more in the image of God.

A second response is the awareness that as persons created in God's image, each person is given unique capabilities which can be developed and used in fulfilling God's intention in creation. Such gifts may be in special personal qualities—the "fruits of the Spirit" in Galatians 5:22-23: love, joy, peace, long-suffering, gentleness, goodness . . . with which to facilitate the formation of another person in Christ. They may also be particular interests, skills, and capabilities that may be further developed through education and training and thus into particular occupations that contribute to the welfare of all God's people. Our calling— our vocation—is to image God in carrying out God's intention in the world. We can do this in many different settings as we express God's love to others. In so doing we extend the presence of God in the world.

God has intervened in a personal way, most notably in sending Jesus Christ to earth to accomplish God's intention in creation. God has also chosen to use those who have committed themselves to Jesus Christ as servants to carry out those intentions. Our response then is to be and become an expression of God's love in the world, helping our neighbor find wholeness, peace, justice, and hope. We will want to discover the unique gifts that God has given and develop that giftedness as a service to God and our fellow human beings.

The teen years are a time of exploration and discovery of identity. Exploring interests and discovering capabilities is an essential part of this process. Effective youth ministry will assist young persons in the discovery and development of their capabilities and will also help them test the variety of ways that their gifts can be used to extend God's presence in the world.

If we truly believe that youth are created to live in the image of God, we can see that they are worthy of our time, energy, and love. We will, however, want to communicate that love in ways that help them be awakened to God's work within. In particular, this will mean that we will view youth as persons who can be responsible "for working out their own salvation in fear and trembling," in growing awareness that it is Christ who is working within.

But this does not mean that we will stand back and just let things happen as they will. Rather, we will be assertive in using every setting available to walk with them in a wide variety of experiences that will awaken them to God's image within. The next chapter will outline specific goals for youth ministry from this perspective.

Part III: Ministry

We have laid the foundation for our project to rebuild youth ministry. We looked at youth and noted their sometimes frantic search for significance. They want to know that they are truly important to someone, which, in turn, they hope will make them feel better deep inside.

Many influencers and persuaders badger youth constantly with claims of a sure, magic solution to relieve this painful struggle. Too often, this is at the expense of the youth themselves. Whatever significance it brings is short lived. Rather than giving lasting significance, the solutions are little more than ways to give greater wealth or power to the influencers and persuaders themselves.

The church is also an influencer and persuader. But it will be totally different from all the others if it is to help youth find true significance. It will take a stance in favor of young people. It will never take advantage of nor manipulate them for its own purposes. Indeed, the church will be a community of faith in which young persons will be encouraged and helped to develop their own abilities, convictions, and values focused on faith in Christ. They will then be capable of making their own decisions. But, even more, they will be able to find true significance.

We can now turn toward the structure in our reconstruction project. In our blueprint we list the building materials needed for the structure and how these can fit together. However, just as each young person is unique, so must each congregation finally piece together its own unique youth ministry program. A youth ministry program begins with a *clear vision and purpose* on which *goals* can be based. It then considers the *settings in the congregation* where the goals can be carried out. In this final part we consider these important structural elements for rebuilding youth ministry.

•Chapter 7 outlines a *vision, purpose, and goals* for congregational youth ministry.

•Chapter 8 addresses *six key principles* for youth ministry programming.

•Chapter 9 describes *settings in the congregation* that can be used in programming for ministry.

•Chapter 10 outlines a *structure—the Youth Ministry Leadership Committee*—that congregations can develop to coordinate the ministry in the various settings.

Chapter 7: CONGREGATIONAL YOUTH MINISTRY: vision, purpose, and goals

The purpose of congregational youth ministry is to provide both an atmosphere and specific experiences that will welcome and integrate youth into the community of faith and facilitate their being and becoming unique expressions of God's love in the world.

The most important part of developing a blueprint happens before anything is ever put on paper. This may be the most difficult part of the whole project. The architect listens carefully to the owners of the proposed building and hears their vision for the future use of the new or rebuilt structure. When the vision is clear, the purposes and goals emerge almost naturally from it.

It is no different with youth ministry. Too frequently those who work with congregational youth ministry become so wrapped up in planning activities that they fail to ever give thought to a vision, purpose, and goals for what they are doing in their ministry with youth.

Vision and purpose

Ministry with youth takes place in many different places. In this book we are concerned particularly with youth ministry in the congregation. While the information in this chapter may have implications for youth ministry as it takes place in other contexts, such as the private Christian high school or in Christian camping, the primary emphasis here is on youth ministry in the congregation.

The first part of our work looked at the needs of the individual young person who is the primary concern of any youth ministry. Then we looked at the congregation as the larger context in which the needs are met. Our vision for youth ministry grows out of these understandings. This vision will be that each young person finds significance through the development of an identity founded in a commitment to being and becoming a unique expression of God's love in the world. We can state this vision as follows:

> The vision of a congregational youth ministry sees the congregation as the primary context for youth to discover their identity as persons created in God's image who are called to be unique expressions of God's love in the world.

This vision points us toward the highest ideal for our efforts in congregational youth ministry. It helps us know something of the ultimate aim of those efforts, capturing what we would most deeply desire for the congregation as well as for the programs that it develops to assist youth toward living that vision. It also points us toward the purpose of those programs:

> The purpose of congregational youth ministry is to provide both an atmosphere and specific experiences that will welcome and integrate youth into the community of faith and facilitate their being and becoming unique expressions of God's love in the world through a dynamic disciplined relationship with Christ.

These statements recognize that the adolescent years are both a time of being and becoming. During these years of identity formation, the community of faith must provide for youth a home—an environment—where they can feel safe. It will be a place where they can be themselves as well as be encouraged in their being and becoming unique expressions of God's love in the world in the midst of many other competing influencers and persuaders.

For the congregation to provide such a safe home it needs to be attentive to the *atmosphere* that is the congregation's life together. This includes the values that are lived by its members, the attitudes expressed, and the lifestyle demonstrated. Significant messages are communicated to youth as they observe the congregation's life together. Much of this is nonverbal communication, opening the possibility of much miscommunication and misunderstanding. If these are dealt with openly and honestly in the congregation, there is much potential for growth together. If hidden or denied, it can hinder and frustrate the congregation's ministry with youth a great deal.

However, atmosphere alone is not adequate to carry out the above purpose. It will be complemented by *experiences* which give youth opportunities to talk of faith in their own words and language. In congregational youth ministry, a range of structured programs will be planned and carried out where young persons can ask how faith relates to their life. It will be a place where youth will be challenged to new understandings.

Young persons will develop their abilities as decision makers in congregations that provide such an atmosphere and experiences. They will become critics of their culture who are able to find the truth in the face of all the messages of the influencers and persuaders. They will be able to know which messages are consistent with the way of Jesus Christ and which are not. Within the loving support of the community of faith, their growth and development will be facilitated as they integrate those that are consistent with the way of Jesus Christ. They will also have the power to reject those that are not.

All of this will have as its cornerstone a dynamic, disciplined relationship with Christ. This relationship will grow out of a commitment to Jesus Christ, who in his death and resurrection provided forgiveness for sin and a new life. This relationship with Christ will be dynamic, that is, growing, deepening, and becoming more disciplined. This will not be for its own sake, but to the end of being and becoming unique expressions of God's love in the world.

Our vision and purpose statements also provide a focus for evaluation of the congregation's ministry with youth: Are we as a community of faith providing such a setting where youth are finding their identity as persons created in God's image? Do our congregational life in general and our specific youth ministry programs assist youth to make their decisions out of a meaningful faith commitment? Does it truly help them live more and more as unique expressions of God's love in the world through a dynamic relationship with Jesus Christ?

Goals

Vision and purpose statements help us see the broader picture of an integrated congregational youth ministry. However, to have meaning, these statements must be broken down into specific goals. These goals will guide the development of programs in the various settings through which the congregation walks with its young persons.

We have noted that the primary task of the adolescent years is the formation of identity. Consequently, every goal of congregational youth ministry is concerned with the *formation of identity*. Within this larger, comprehensive task three areas can be identified, each of which makes a special contribution to the formation of identity: (1) *relationships*, (2) *values and philosophy of life*, and (3) *occupations exploration*.

The following illustration uses a Venn diagram from mathematics, suggesting that each of these areas is part of the global task of identity formation. The three overlapping circles within the larger circle indicate that each area—Relationships, Philosophy of Life, and Occupations Exploration—has its own particular agenda. Each, however, is also related to the others. The directions taken in one area affect what is decided in the others.

Youth in the church are not the only ones to experience this process. Indeed, it is a process through which every

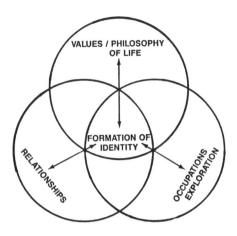

young person goes. Our concern is to help youth through it in the best possible way. Our premise is that youth will find their way through this process best in a caring, supportive congregation. The vision and purpose that have been outlined will guide these congregations as they develop programs that respond to the deepest needs of their youth.

The following list of goals has been developed to remind congregational youth ministry program planners of the wide range of issues and concerns that needs to be addressed. The length and scope of the list help us understand the size and complexity of our youth ministry task. However, planners should attempt to find ways to incorporate each goal into programming during the teen years for each young person. In doing this, each youth will be offered the needed resources for decision making that can lead to a life of deepest significance.

Formation of identity

The formation of a personal identity is the overarching task of the adolescent. A personal identity is shaped as the young person makes decisions and commitments. Such choices, large or small, insignificant or significant, are not isolated but, rather, build on others. This suggests how complex the decision making process really is. For many young persons it requires great effort because the pool of information on which choices are made is vast, coming to the young person with great intensity. Ultimately, this task is the formation of the "heart." It will determine how one will view the world and the stance that will be taken in understanding one's place in it.

1. Youth will come to know themselves as persons created in God's own image and therefore of ultimate value. They will see that being created in God's image is the only lasting foundation for knowing their identity and therefore, their significance. They will understand that other ways such as popularity, instant gratification, power, and security as proclaimed by many entertainers, buyers and sellers, politicians, and militarists make similar, but ultimately false, claims to be the basis for identity and significance.

2. Youth will understand the meaning of sin as an ever-present option that separates us from God. They will understand sin in both a personal and corporate sense and discover that through God's gracious love, as demonstrated by God's redemptive work in Christ, forgiveness, and restoration of relationship are freely offered to those who respond.

3. Youth will develop personal and corporate disciplines that facilitate their ongoing growth and development in living in a dynamic, disciplined relationship with Christ. These may include journaling, meditation and reflection, silence and prayer, and regular participation in congregational worship.

4. Youth will be grounded in hope built on faith which will allow them to live creatively—even in the face of the threat of nuclear war and the annihilation of the human race, and with a hope that renders meaningless all other bases for hope such as wealth, power, or prestige.

Relationships
Relationships demand a significant portion of an adolescent's thought and energy. Youth have developed and are continuing to form a style of relating to themselves and to others which can greatly affect their feelings. Through re-

flection on these relationship patterns, the young person will be given tools for the development of a healthy relationship to self (self-esteem) and for positive relationships with others.

1. Youth will gain insight into their own development, initially as persons dependent on parents for nearly all of life's needs, now coming into a time of life of greater independence from parents which includes taking more personal responsibility for decisions. In this they will take their place as responsible family members, doing their part to maintain healthy, helpful family relationships.

2. Youth will learn to communicate in helpful ways, particularly with family members closest to them, but with others as well. Through this youth will be helped to understand interdependence—giving and receiving helpful wisdom and counsel to and from others.

3. Youth will develop healthy relationships with peers and choose those persons as friends who will provide helpful, mutual support, and from whom they will enjoy acceptance and love. They will be able to test their ideas with these friends. From among them special relationships may develop that could eventuate in a long-term commitment such as marriage.

4. Youth will develop healthy relationships with persons from other generations and value these relationships as sources of support that will provide much wisdom for decisions that they must make.

5. Youth will learn skills that will help them work through times of conflict with family, peers, and others. These skills will prove useful not only in interpersonal relationships but in understanding conflict between nations and ideologies.

Values/philosophy of life

The values and the basic orientation (philosophy) to life itself that one adopts grow out of a wide range of learning and experience. This includes faith understandings, becoming informed about the world and its peoples, and awareness of the natural world. Out of such values and life philosophy, commitments are fashioned for meaningful, purposeful living.

1. Youth will learn the story of God's repeated attempts to be in relationship with humankind through study of the Scriptures and through study of the history of the Christian church.

2. Youth will make personal commitments to Christ at the level of their understanding. They will unite through baptism with the church as the community of faith in membership at the age of mature, owned faith, supported by instruction (catechism) for baptism and church membership. They will develop a sensitivity to the Holy Spirit as a resource and guide for living out their commitment to Christ.

3. Youth will become active participants in personal and corporate worship in recognition of, and as response to, a loving God who is creator, sustainer, and protector of all life.

4. Youth will learn about the contemporary church in "Jerusalem, Judea, Samaria, and the uttermost part of the earth" (Acts 1:8). They will learn of its mission and ministry and will become involved in a personal ministry of their own.

5. Youth will learn about other religious traditions, both within the larger Christian community as well as other world religions and cults. In so doing they will come to more fully understand the particular emphases of the Anabaptist/believers' church tradition, and discover what it has in common as well as where it differs from these other traditions.

6. Youth will know their whole being as a "temple of the Holy Spirit." They will care for themselves through personal habits that nourish their being and avoid those that hurt and destroy. In particular, they will cherish their sexuality, understanding it as a gift of the Creator that permeates their entire existence.

7. Youth will come to see themselves as part of a global

family, integrally connected to all peoples of the earth in the struggle for survival and happiness.

8. Youth will gain, from their emerging faith, understandings on that which is needed or essential for meaningful existence as opposed to that which is non-essential (that is, needs versus wants).

9. Youth will develop understanding of and appreciation for the world in which they live, and discern how to be caretakers and managers of all the resources of God's creation. This includes stewardship education for using financial and personal resources as well as those of the natural world.

Occupations exploration

Every person is uniquely gifted by the Creator. The search for how to meaningfully invest one's time and energy as an adult in a particular occupation begins to be shaped during the childhood and adolescent years. During adolescence youth can explore their own personal giftedness and be given opportunities to test their interests and abilities. They will also explore ways to further develop their interests and abilities as the basis for potential meaningful vocation.

1. Youth will develop their interests and abilities and venture into new or related areas as a means of testing their personal giftedness, and view these as possible areas of occupational choice. One important dimension of this is development of leadership skills.

2. Youth will be exposed to the varieties of occupational possibilities available today. They will be encouraged to see their life work as service in response to God's creative and redemptive work and be helped to consider which options are consistent with their developing interests and abilities and with their growing faith and lifestyle directions.

3. Youth will be given tools needed to explore specific occupations, including the need for training, which may include higher education. They will be encouraged to attend church-related colleges, not only to train for a specific

occupation but also to further their understanding of God and the world from an Anabaptist/believers' church perspective.

It hardly needs to be said that these goals represent extremely high ideals. Each is written in terms of a desired outcome. Some would argue that the outcomes are too idealistic and are therefore impossible to ever fully achieve. Perhaps this is the case.

But, in youth ministry we must never give in to what seems to be realistic. With God's help, we can in congregational youth ministry take giant steps toward the sum total of these goals, that is, helping each youth be and become a unique expression of God's love in the world.

Chapter 8:   YOUTH MINISTRY PROGRAMMING: six general considerations

In a community of faith it is important to accept youth as they are.

With the vision, purpose, and goals of our rebuilding task now in focus, we are ready to begin drawing our blueprint which we can follow in building our congregational youth ministry. At least seven specific settings where the congregation touches the lives of youth can be identified.

Before looking at these settings in detail, however, we want to look at six general principles to keep in mind as the blueprint takes shape. They might be compared to the basic principles of architecture and design that are necessary in the construction of any building.

These general principles include:

1. *The individual within the community is the focus of youth ministry.*

2. *Positive relationships are key to effective youth ministry.*

3. *Special events in the young person's life provide unique youth ministry opportunities.*

4. *Youth can learn through reflection on their experiences.*

5. *Leadership training can take place in all youth ministry efforts.*

6. *Every setting in the congregation where youth's lives are touched is an opportunity for youth ministry.*

Let us examine each of these more closely.

1. *The individual within the community is the focus of youth ministry.* In Western culture there is much talk of individual freedom, initiative, and achievement. Ironically, however, we more typically work with groups. Many times the individual gets lost unless she or he is particularly assertive. Our educational approach groups persons by age in grades. The person who, for whatever reason, does not fit may be considered an oddball by peers or may receive little individual help or encouragement from teachers. This may be because they do not fit the stereotypic beauty queen image or they may be seen as having little potential because of low academic achievement or negative behavior patterns.

On the other hand, some young persons with particular abilities may be singled out and may become the focus of uncomfortably high expectations. The athletic jock may be expected to bring home victory after victory and may receive special favors from teachers so that he can continue to play even though his academic performance may leave much to be desired. Persons with certain personal qualities or leadership gifts may be expected to be a role model beyond the youth's capabilities. Any individual attention tends to be only in relation to what it will do for the larger group and not in terms of what it is doing to the individual.

Some congregations are also guilty of thinking only in terms of the group. Here all youth are seen primarily as part of the youth group where the youth group sponsors are expected to be the primary members who relate to them. The group is the vehicle through which the ministry of the congregation to its youth is channeled. Some young persons, however, receive little, if any, personal attention from sponsors. This is especially true if they feel themselves to be on the fringes of the group, do not enjoy the activities planned, or tend to be quiet and not very assertive. Furthermore, busy sponsors simply do not have enough time to relate on a close personal level with each youth.

Grouping can simplify programming. However, ministry with youth must never lose sight of the individuals who make up the group. We have already pointed to the uniqueness of each young person and the importance of developing at her or his own pace. Each has special gifts and needs. This uniqueness makes it essential that we look at each person as an individual within the group and never only as a member of the group.

Implications
Persons working with programming. First of all, the youth program will find ways to help each youth personally reflect on questions, develop understandings and values, and make commitments. Some youth will be comfortable doing this in a group setting. But many will not. This may be due to time limitations but more likely fear of what others might think. Consequently, congregations will find ways to enter into individual dialogue with each young person beyond that which takes place in the home. A number of the settings described in chapter 8 lend themselves to such individual dialogue.

Secondly, the faith journey of each youth will be taken very seriously. This means that congregations will provide in their program opportunities for interaction and dialogue for every young person with at least one other person with whom he or she feels comfortable. This will open ways for the congregation to come to know youth an individuals, including awareness of where they are in their faith journeys.

A father recently told me of his son's return to regular church attendance, even on Sunday evening. He went on to say that this son's girlfriend was able to do what he as a parent could not. I wondered whether the fellow would continue going to church should the relationship end. I wanted to believe that his interest in church was a sign of interest in spiritual things. But secretly I doubted that this was more than a way to keep dating this certain girl.

This suggests that the motives for going to church vary widely among youth. Nor are they at the same place in their faith journey. Some, like the fellow above, will come with a marginal commitment to the church. They will show up at a youth group social activity but never for a serious Bible study. They may attend church only enough to satisfy the church league rules for participation on the church's softball or basketball team.

On the other hand, we see youth whose behavior and attitude reflect a strong, deep commitment to Christ and the church. They attend regularly all youth ministry activities, including congregational worship. They will prepare in advance for discussions in youth Sunday school class and enter into honest dialogue about how their faith can be expressed in daily living. They will care in concrete ways for others in their group and reach out to others who may be hurting or lonely. They will take stands against harmful practices that may be the popular thing to do.

The two groups of youth that I have just described are two quite different extremes on a continuum that represents faith commitment. We might question whether some in the first group demonstrate any commitment at all. And some in the latter group may be just putting on an act.

But the fact is that unless we can look at each teenager who enters our youth ministry programming as an individual, we risk the possibility of losing an opportunity to encourage and challenge them to growth and a deeper faith commitment. Furthermore, unless youth ministry planners have some awareness of the individuals and their faith experience, their efforts may not connect with the needs of their youth.

In a community of faith it is important to accept youth as they are. In doing this we will recognize that most youth will express differing degrees of interest at different times in their lives. We will understand that the faith journey for youth (and for all of us) is more typically one of peaks and valleys. There will be those peak times when new insights give us renewed enthusiasm and commitment. But much of our time will be spent in the valley where growth is much slower and commitment sometimes seems to waver.

Observing and considering where a person is on the faith journey may seem to be judging unfairly. Such an assessment, to be sure, must be done humbly and prayerfully and carried out in appropriate dialogue with the individual young person. This is the only way that it is appropriate to encourage and challenge a young person to a deeper commitment. It must be done in the spirit of encouraging growth rather than putting a person in a box out of which, it is assumed, the youth will never come.

2. *Positive relationships are key to effective youth ministry.* In chapter 3 we noted that friendships are very important to young persons. Congregations that see themselves as a community of faith will sincerely want their youth to feel welcome. They will seek to build a network of warm, caring relationships around each one. This will include both peers and persons from other generations.

This is becoming increasingly difficult as congregations do not meet as frequently as they once did. Even youth groups do not meet as often as was once the case, due to the increasingly busy schedules of the youth. Consequently intentional group-building activities need to be planned as part of many different settings.

Youth Sunday school teachers could once assume that their students knew each other well because of the strength of relationships built in other settings. More recently, however, we find that some youth hardly relate to others in the congregation. They may be from a distant part of the city, attend a high school where there are no other persons from their congregation, and therefore only see other youth from their congregation on Sunday morning. Through no fault of their own, they are on the fringe of things. Since Sunday school seems to work best when youth have some acquaintance with each other, it is essential that the teacher give attention to group building as part of the total teaching process.

Emphasizing warm, caring relationships is also critical because of the competition that surrounds each young person. There is competition for grades, for popularity, for friends, and for the prestigious positions in their schools. There is competition for scholarships, sometimes for jobs, and for the nicest, best things. There is competition between schools, especially in athletics but also increasingly in every other program: music, speech, and overall academic achievement.

Competition can bring out the best in a person, but it can also be demoralizing to those who are on the losing end most of the time. The congregation must provide a place where the young person does not need to compete to have her or his needs met. It must be a place where the individual can receive unconditional love and acceptance.

Working carefully and purposefully is even more important when thinking of building relationships between the generations who are in the congregation. Times when youth and adults are together are often those where people look at the backs of each other's heads. Little face-to-face interaction between youth and adults happens in some congregations. Yet intergenerational relationships offer the great potential for the unconditional love and acceptance that youth so much need.

Some congregations have tried intentional group mixing activities in both informal and formal settings. One congregation numbered each table for some of their carry-in meals. Persons drew a number from a box as they took their food and ate their meal at the numbered table. This provided for mixing the congregation as they ate, often with a variety of ages at each table.

Others work at intergenerational relationships through developing mentoring relationships. These special relationships provide the possibility for one adult, other than a parent, to give each young person unconditional love and acceptance.

Youth desire and need both positive peer and intergenerational relationships. The church can provide both in ways that will build and strengthen commitment to Christ and the church.

3. *Special events in the young person's life provide unique youth ministry opportunities.* One significant aspect of a youth ministry that takes seriously each individual young person is a recognition of special occasions in their lives. Outstanding achievement in sports, music, or academics often are noted in the local media with pictures or articles. Some congregations post these clippings in a prominent place for church members to see.

Unfortunately, those who cannot make such outstanding achievements never get recognized. Consequently it is important that congregations find ways to recognize the specialness of each young person, not only those with above average athletic or intellectual ability. Several occasions lend themselves well to such recognition and affirmation.

Baptism. Of all the occasions where special recognition can be given, the most important is the time when the young person is baptized. While the age at baptism varies a great deal in our congregations, in most it signals the beginning of formal church membership. Increasingly it is also a time when the young person takes greater responsibility for personal faith. No longer is faith largely an imitation of the parents' faith. Because of this it can be celebrated with joy.

Unfortunately, in many congregations it continues to be routine, celebrated in a group that has recently completed its catechism or instruction class. Some congregations, however, are planning a special, individual baptismal service for each young person. It may take place in a Sunday evening service, on Sunday morning, or at another time. The young person being baptized participates in the planning of the service and is invited to make a special contribution to it. In one congregation, the young persons have shared gifts such as special music, liturgical dance, a reading, and a description of artwork at the baptismal service. It also included an opportunity for the youth being baptized to share a brief statement of her or his own understanding of faith and personal commitment to Christ.

Birthdays. Having a birthday is obviously a common experience to everyone. Birthdays can be listed and each person can be recognized in some special way as near as possible to the birthday. This could happen through listing the birthdays for the following week in the church bulletin, or sending a carefully-selected card from the congregation signed by the pastor and youth group leaders. Birthdays might also be recognized in a youth group meeting or a celebration for all persons having birthdays during a particular month. The ways that congregations can celebrate birthdays is limited only by its imagination.

Driver's license. Obtaining a driver's license signals a new phase in the experience of most young persons. There is a new freedom to go and come when one has "wheels." There is also a new sense of responsibility as the teen drives away in what is likely one of the family's largest investments. Along with this new freedom and responsibility there is also a new sense of power in taking command of the "horses" under the hood.

In many provinces and states the legal driving age is sixteen. Whatever the age, youth ministry can recognize this special time in the life of the youth. It can pledge its care and love as the youth enters this new phase. Some congregations recognize this time by giving the young person a symbolic key or key chain along with a special prayer for sound judgment and protection in driving.

Beginning of mentoring relationship. Some congregations are choosing to establish a mentoring relationship for each interested young person. More complete background and description of mentoring relationships is given in the following chapter.

The beginning of this relationship is a significant step in broadening the youth's support system to include another adult beyond the parents. It provides a unique opportunity for congregational affirmation and blessing of the special friendship between the young person and the adult chosen as mentor. Although this can take place anytime in the youth's experience, the twelfth birthday is a good time for this special relationship to begin. Special recognition around this time reminds us of the Jewish tradition of bar mitzvah for boys or bas mitzvah for girls.

Congregations often plan for recognition of new mentoring relationships during Sunday morning worship. The pastor or mentor program coordinator may introduce the young person and the mentor and offer selected words of encouragement and support to them. Parents of the young person are often asked to stand with the youth and mentor as a signal of their support for the relationship. It is also an opportunity for them to acknowledge the support that they as parents are given through the time and the energy the mentor invests in their daughter or son.

Graduation. Graduation from high school is a significant milestone in a teenager's life. The obligations of schooling are now completed and greater freedom in using time is now assumed. Congregations that have taken seriously their responsibility to help youth in their decision making will see this as a time to recognize and affirm the decisions that they have made for work, further schooling, service, or any of many other options.

One congregation recognizes this time by presenting a special coffee mug to each graduate on a Sunday morning. This is followed by a special carry-in dinner where each young person is given time to tell the congregation of plans that have been made.

4. *Youth can learn through reflection on their experiences.* Teens, like children, learn best from experience as opposed to simply discussing or talking about ideas and concepts. But teens, unlike children, possess the new capability to think abstractly and to generalize. They can now take learnings from experiences, build on them, and apply them to other circumstances.

Children generally see their experiences as unrelated to any other experiences. For example, children can be told about justice and injustice, but unless it has taken place in some way in their experience, such as a friend being treated unfairly, they will have difficulty understanding it. They are, for the most part, unable to take learnings from one experience and apply them to another set of circumstances. They think concretely, in terms of what is immediately available to their senses.

Adults may be able to discuss a wide range of ideas and concepts and learn a great deal from discussions even without the benefit of having been personally involved. But teens are similar to children in that learning happens best when they can be personally involved as opposed to just talking about a particular topic. Different from children, however, is their ability to reflect on and name particular learnings from those experiences which can be applied to others. Teens can understand injustice when it happens in their personal experience and can use those learnings to recognize it in the circumstances of persons whom they may not know personally. This ability also allows them to generalize from their experiences and develop ideals of what is good or bad, right or wrong.

Consequently, it is important to build on their experiences as an avenue for learning and growth. This can happen in two ways. First of all, special experiences can be planned within any youth ministry setting that may not be part of their normal, day-to-day experiences. A weekend visit to the city to see poverty and circumstances of injustice will provide for much greater learning than a discussion in youth group of poverty in the city.

One congregation plans an annual service experience in another country where the youth come face-to-face with conditions that often exist in Third World countries. Another congregation tries to make a heritage tour possible for each young person. On the excursion the youth see firsthand the places where their denomination originated and discuss the circumstances which gave rise to the beliefs which they hold. Activities in the classroom that simulate circumstances again prove to be better learning experiences than just talking about it.

These special experiences do provide unique opportunities for learning in working with youth. Too often, however, we miss opportunities for even greater learning when we fail to see their normal, day-to-day experiences as similar opportunities. Their relationships with friends, what they are learning in school and how it fits or may not fit with their faith understandings, their participation in music, drama, athletics—all these provide significant opportunities for learning and growth.

The most significant learning, however, from these experiences comes through their ability to reflect on and generalize about them. Seeing firsthand the poverty that exists in a Third-World country gives an excellent opportunity to help the young persons ask how they might be contributing to those circumstances through their own lifestyles, even though they live many miles away. It also is an excellent opportunity to encourage them to begin to make commitments that can make the world a better place, not only for those whom they became acquainted with but for all people.

The fact that youth do generalize from their experiences is illustrated in many ways. Their beliefs about their own significance often arise out of their inability to meet a certain ideal in one particular experience, such as in academics, which is generalized to all other areas of their lives. For instance, a teen may say, If I can't make straight A's, I'm not good for anything. Their newfound ability to put themselves "in the other person's shoes" may give them a certainty about what others are thinking which may be far from what the others are truly thinking.

Youth typically do their reflecting alone or with peers. They may miss the larger perspective which comes through dialogue with persons who have lived longer. This is extremely important because of the tendency to be overly hard on oneself if one cannot see the larger view.

However, the *way* this larger perspective is presented to youth by adults in their lives is very crucial. Too often it is given as "this is the way it is" or in a judgmental way. This does not help the youth consider alternative ways of viewing his or her experience. It does little more than turn the youth off and stifle further communication.

This suggests that listening is very important in youth-adult communication. Indeed, listening is the single most important skill for persons who work with youth to develop. It is through careful listening that we encourage youth to express themselves and to process their experiences. It is only through appropriate listening on the adult's part that youth will want to invite the wisdom and observations of those who are older. Michael Warren sums this up in a very powerful way when he says "that the key organ for the (person) dealing with teens is not the big mouth but the big ear. There is an important catechetical task of listening, of evocative listening, the kind of listening that encourages others to come to speech" ("Can Liturgy Speak to Young People" in *Readings and Resources for Youth Ministry*, Winona, Minn.: St. Mary's Press, 1987, p. 33).

5. *Leadership training can take place in all youth ministry efforts.* Leadership training is an underlying concern of every aspect of ministry with youth in the congregation. Youth are the church of today. Nevertheless, an important part of youth ministry must consider that these persons

will one day assume leadership in the congregation and the larger denomination. Consequently, leadership training must be part and parcel of the church's youth ministry program.

Youth ministry offers a variety of settings where young persons can develop their leadership abilities. In leadership training the church gives attention to developing leaders to provide for its own needs in congregations as well as its churchwide agencies and institutions. It will also keep in mind that such training will provide caring, positive leadership in many other secular settings. Young persons whose level of commitment gives them some understanding of the meaning of being an expression of God's love in the world can be a good influence in schools, clubs, and other social contexts. Similarly, as they enter the world of work, sensitive leadership on the job can provide for happier, more wholesome employees as well as employee-employer relations.

Too often, well-meaning sponsors or others who work with youth take over leadership of activities, robbing the young persons of opportunities to develop their leadership skills and abilities. In giving the youth greater responsibility, sponsors may see the youth fumble and even fail miserably. But even in such circumstances, sponsors can play a valuable role as they help pick up the pieces, reflect on the experience, and think through how things might be handled differently in the future.

Apprentice-type arrangements can also be established. A young person can walk closely with an adult leader for a given block to time to observe and to participate in planning and carrying out a particular task. One pastor discussed the sermon for the following Sunday with several young persons each week. He took them along on some pastoral calls in homes and hospitals, and worked together with them in a number of the administrative tasks.

Sensitive, caring, assertive leaders are desperately needed in our society today. The church can be a place where persons are equipped for such leadership.

6. *Every setting in the congregation where youth's lives are touched is an opportunity for youth ministry.* In the past, congregations have assumed that the youth group will be the primary setting where youth ministry goals will be carried out. Some of these congregations place the entire responsibility for meeting these goals in one person—the youth pastor—or the youth sponsors. We have already pointed to the difficulties some congregations face in such a program- or pastor-centered approach.

If we are to be faithful in ministry with youth, today's circumstances demand that every setting in the congregation where the lives of youth are touched be used to carry out these goals. This assumes that the youth group will be only one component of its youth ministry programming and that congregations will learn to see other settings as places where important youth ministry also occurs. They will also make every attempt to coordinate planning for and content of each of these settings so that they will provide for a coordinated, holistic program. Thus they will implement what we might call an Integrated Congregational Youth Ministry.

In the next chapter we consider seven specific settings in the congregation on which to build such an Integrated Congregational Youth Ministry.

Chapter 9: INTEGRATED CONGREGATIONAL YOUTH MINISTRY: seven settings

The congregation, as a community of faith, offers at least seven specific, formal settings where the lives of youth are touched and ministry can take place.

Ministry with youth in the congregation takes place in many different ways and in a variety of settings. Some of the best ministry likely happens in the informal settings— the casual chat between an adult and a young person after a service, an invitation to the youth to spend an evening in a home playing, talking, and eating, a group of youth getting together for pizza and having a good time discussing issues of significant concern, or youth and adults playing together on the church softball team.

These and many other informal interactions must be noted as significant youth ministry. The congregation, however, as a community of faith offers at least seven specific, formal settings where the lives of youth are touched and ministry can take place. These include:

1. *Congregational worship*
2. *Youth Sunday school*
3. *Youth group*
4. *Catechism (instruction for baptism and church membership)*
5. *Mentoring relationships*

6. *Peer ministries*
7. *Family life*

We want to look at each of these areas individually in terms of their potential for carrying out our stated purpose of providing "both and atmosphere and specific experiences that will welcome and integrate youth into the family of God and facilitate their becoming unique expressions of God's love in the world." While the seven settings are listed individually, the most effective youth ministry will see them as parts of a larger, coordinated effort. This is what we want to call an Integrated Congregational Youth Ministry.

Congregational worship

In most congregations, more youth attend Sunday morning worship service than any other activity. That the time that the congregation gathers for worship—typically on Sunday morning—is a youth ministry setting is often not seriously considered. Some youth come for no other reason than that they are forced to come by their parents. Others are there simply to be with their church friends and, as a group, hold securely to the bench farthest back on the right side. Still others who come are eager to receive something from the service, willing to be personally involved whenever they are invited. They listen attentively and participate actively in all aspects of the service.

With the varying levels of commitment that young people bring to the worship service, it is a significant challenge to find ways that this setting can be used to carry out our youth ministry goals. At one level, it can do so simply by providing a place where youth can come to feel part of a group—a community. This is of vital importance to many.

Young persons can express their identity with and feel a sense of belonging to the community of faith through their participation in corporate worship. They can also participate in congregational worship as a means of expressing their response to God in the context of the faith community. They also gain greater understanding of God and God's activity in the past, present, and future through corporate worship.

If congregational worship is to be an effective setting for ministry to all ages, including youth, it will be viewed as an intergenerational experience and as such will include elements that appeal to each age group involved. The following suggestions illustrate ways that will draw youth into the worship experience and increase their ownership and participation in it.

1. *Appeal to both intellect and feeling.* Perhaps no other age group maintains the intensity of feeling more than adolescents. Consequently, it is important that worship experiences appeal to feelings as well as intellect. For example, music is an important means of expressing feeling for youth. Congregational worship should occasionally include music which most appeals to youth such as Scripture songs or songs with a beat. Youth groups that have musical talent could be invited to share special music, perhaps a piece with a more modern or rock sound.

2. *Give youth responsibilities in worship leadership.* Music is one area where youth are often willing to be involved in the worship experience. This may be in special music as a youth group or by participation in an intergenerational choir. Sharing in worship leading, ushering, reading Scripture, liturgical dance, and drama are other ways to involve youth. Pastors might also find ways to incorporate youth into sermon preparation and delivery such as in dialogue sermons.

3. *Appoint youth representative(s) on the worship planning committee.* A young person or two can be appointed to serve on the worship planning committee. This person will represent the interests of youth but also might be seen in an apprentice role. The young person would assist the worship planner or leader, thereby gaining some valuable experience in leadership training.

4. *Be sensitive to various age groups in sermons.* Youth, with their ability to generalize and think abstractly,

can understand the sermon. However, the pastor should be sensitive to the youth, particularly in the words and illustrations used. The vocabulary of the youth is often limited, especially when it comes to theological terms. Too often youth simply "turn off" when words seem to be over their heads. Pastors and others who are preaching can avoid this by writing a draft of the sermon and examining it carefully for such language.

In preparing the message, the preacher might also take time to discuss the central concept with a group of youth to find ways to express it in language that youth will understand. The use of a transparency with overhead projection with an outline of the key points can also be useful in helping youth maintain interest and attention. Using audiovisuals occasionally may also be helpful.

5. *Have special youth emphases Sundays.* Every worship experience of the congregation should be planned with the interests and needs of the youth in mind. However, within the overall calendar the congregation may want to include a special annual emphasis on youth. This may be one designated Sunday or, better yet, a week-long emphasis.

For example, a youth emphasis might include a youth group "live-in" for the youth at the church's meetinghouse. Each evening a different group of adults would be selected to plan and serve the group its evening meal. These adults could stay after the meal for a brief worship time or dialogue around a concern of mutual interest.

The week could culminate in several special events. On Saturday evening the youth could host the entire congregation for a picnic meal and program. The program might be a variety show format that would feature the youth. Others from the congregation could also be invited to share their talents.

Finally, the Sunday morning service could include special involvement by the youth. A committee of youth and sponsors would work in close cooperation with the pastor or worship planners to put together the service. Several young persons could be worship leaders, the youth group could offer special music, and several might assist in presenting the sermon which would address a topic of special interest to youth.

It has been said that what a person is willing to invest in a worship service determines what that person will get out of it. Youth with a high degree of commitment find elements in congregational worship that help them grow in their faith because they are willing to be involved as active participants or because pastors and worship planners are tuned into their needs. Some youth do appreciate congregational worship in spite of little or no effort to include them or to make the service meaningful or appealing to them. Many more youth could be drawn into worship if congregational leaders would pay careful attention to their interests and needs as services are planned and carried out.

Youth Sunday school

The Sunday school class, like congregational worship, typically takes place on Sunday morning. And, like congregational worship, it brings together youth with widely varying degrees of commitment. Some youth want to enter into serious discussion of issues and topics of concern to them during his hour. Others are there only to see friends or because their parents say they must attend.

The varying degrees of commitment represented by the youth present a great challenge for those who are leaders or teachers during this hour. Teachers and serious students are often frustrated by someone more interested in talking with a friend or offering wisecracks when asked a question. Making the education hour primarily a social time with little or no expectation of any learning taking place may meet the needs of those with a low degree of commitment, but will often be very frustrating to those who want more serious discussion.

Traditionally, the Sunday school has been one hour in

length. However, this Sunday school "hour" is often reduced to thirty or forty minutes, especially in those congregations where the worship hour takes place first and frequently lasts longer than the time normally given to it. If a "coffee hour" for the entire congregation is added, there may even be less time.

Poorly prepared curriculum is sometimes a source of frustration for the Sunday school leaders. Another problem is that some teachers are unwilling to put adequate time and effort into preparation, both in training for teaching more generally and for each Sunday's lesson.

Given these circumstances, many congregations have very low expectations of the Sunday school hour. They have given up on it as a time for formal Christian education. Some are choosing to see it as the weekly youth group meeting; it is primarily a time of informal interaction for building relationships among the youth. If any time is left, there may be a brief discussion of a particular topic of interest to the youth or from a prepared curriculum.

Other congregations continue to view the education hour as a very significant time for formal Christian education. They want it to be a time of serious study and discussion of Scripture, of the church and what it believes, or of contemporary concerns of the youth themselves. In this brief time of study and reflection, the youth work together to discover how they can more fully live out their commitment to be unique expressions of God's love in the world.

Some congregations that continue to view the Sunday school primarily as formal Christian education struggle to maintain the young people's interest. This may be because the lecture is the primary teaching method and few youth get involved beyond just being there. These congregations insist on continuing such a pattern because, as they say, there is no other place in the congregation where they will get religious knowledge. The youth may absorb something—at least, they are present.

Congregations that implement an Integrated Congregational Youth Ministry will carefully consider their particular circumstances in deciding how best to use the time given to Sunday school. In most congregations there will be a minimum of two youth classes, one for junior high (grades 7-8) and one for high school (grades 9-12). Some small congregations may choose to combine the groups while larger ones may plan two or more for the high school group.

A key question that will need to be considered, both in forming classes as well as content, is whether the youth have opportunity to build relationships in other settings such as their youth group. If so, the possibility of success in a more formal education approach is much greater than it will be if this is the primary time when the youth are together. Let us look at how Sunday school might happen in both circumstances.

1. *If the Sunday school hour is the primary time when all of the youth are together*, the teacher will be seen more as a leader than a teacher. The youth group sponsors will likely be involved, either as participants or as leaders because this is in reality youth group time. The following elements will need to be included:

(a) *Opportunity for group building and interaction.* Early in the Sunday school year, class time will need to be given to activities that help the youth learn to know each other and hear about each other's experiences. This may happen informally in "sharing" time as individuals report on their experiences in school, work, home, or other activities. It may also happen in more intentionally structured "ice breakers" and get-acquainted activities.

(b) *Youth group business.* If there is no youth group or if it has only a minimum of organization, when the group is together, time will be needed to work out details for any activities that are planned as a group. This may range from announcements to group processing of plans for the next youth activity.

(c) *Study focus.* The above two elements will take priority and consequently take most of the time. However, there may be opportunity for a twenty-to thirty-minute study and learning experience. If a prepared curriculum is used, the teacher will need to choose very carefully a portion of the suggested material with the goal of considering a concept or discussing a concern that can be covered in the brief time available. Frequently there will only be time to introduce the concept or concern or the group will just begin a good discussion when it is time for dismissal.

2. *If there is a strong youth group* and opportunity for relationship building in other settings, the Sunday school hour can be used for more formal Christian education. In such a setting, a curriculum will be used to assure a more systematic study of a particular subject area. Serious attention will be given to the use of appropriate and effective teaching methods. The class period should be at least fifty minutes in length.

The youth group will also provide opportunity for more formal teaching where the focus will primarily be on considering contemporary issues and concerns. The Sunday school will, on the other hand, focus on learning the story of God and God's people throughout history. This will be done through reviewing stories heard during the childhood years and revisioning these, now with adolescent understanding. This will be done in three primary areas:

(a) *Bible study.* One aspect of a study of the Bible will focus on how it came to us and how it is most appropriately interpreted. However, more important will be the actual study of the biblical material with special focus on the life of Jesus through study of the Gospels. The Old Testament will be considered as a backdrop to discover the way God dealt with persons for salvation during that time and as preparatory to Jesus coming into the world. What follows the Gospels in the New Testament will be studied to learn the events and circumstances of the establishment of the church which carries on Jesus' work.

(b) *The study of church history.* It has been said that those who do not learn from their past are doomed to repeat it. The history of the church is filled with many illustrations of how its leaders lost sight of its basic purpose and it became only a shadow of what God intended for it. But the history of the church is also filled with many moments when God broke through to bring freshness and renewal. Of particular importance is the story of the Reformation of the sixteenth century. We are particularly interested in the movements initiated by the Anabaptists and later by Mennonites and Church of the Brethren persons.

A study of the history of the church also includes a major focus on the contemporary church in the world. Youth will become aware of how and where their own denomination is involved in mission and service throughout the world both nationally and internationally. The mission and service involvement of other Christian churches will also be considered. Young persons will develop special awareness of and appreciation for ways that their church cooperates with others.

(c) *Basic doctrines and beliefs of the church.* It is important that youth gain insight and understanding into what it means to be part of the Anabaptist tradition in general and in particular of the Mennonite church or Church of the Brethren. What does this tradition share in common with believers in other denominations? And what are the distinctive beliefs of those who identify with the Anabaptist faith?

Such a focus would help the youth become acquainted with the range of understandings of the Christian life present in their own denomination. It would also include a look at other denominations and their particular emphases as well as becoming acquainted with other religions of the world.

Congregations that use an Integrated Congregational Youth Ministry will need to carefully assess their own special circumstances as they make plans for Sunday school. It is likely that the two approaches outlined earlier will be extremes and the final shape of the experience will fall somewhere between.

One final question must be addressed before leaving the Sunday school setting: If youth do not receive the content of the more formal Christian education approach as suggested above in Sunday school, where will they receive it? The Integrated Congregational Youth Ministry model offers several other possible settings. These might be incorporated into a strengthened and longer catechism (instruction) class. Special week-night classes for interested youth, perhaps including some adults, might also be planned as part of the youth group program.

Youth group

For the past twenty-five years the youth group has been the focal point of youth ministry in many congregations. The youth group has offered a significant resource to each young person as a social setting, a place for reflection and dialogue on many different issues and concerns from a Christian perspective, and a context that encouraged significant spiritual growth. It continues to be of great importance in many congregations.

Other congregations, however, have experienced considerable difficulty in maintaining an active youth group. In some, the primary cause for this is a decreasing number of youth. In others, the cause seems more related to increasing assimilation of the youth into other nonchurch groupings such as school or community. In still others, especially in urban areas, the distance between the homes of the participants makes meeting regularly difficult.

As we noted above in discussing the Sunday school, where it is difficult to maintain an active youth group, the Sunday school time will be very important in building relationships among the youth. The potential for stronger, more healthy peer relationships in the congregation is much greater when it is possible to develop and maintain an active youth group. Consequently, an Integrated Congregational Youth Ministry views the youth group as an important setting where possible. It is often asked how many youth a congregation must have to develop an active youth group. In many respects this depends as much on the ability of the youth present to function as a group as it does on a precise number. In some congregations six to ten youth will function effectively as a group, while others with larger numbers will have more difficulty developing an effective youth group. In general, congregations with fewer than five youth will find it difficult to establish and maintain a youth group. These congregations may need to focus their youth ministry in other settings. Another option would be to combine with youth from another nearby congregation.

In some congregations the youth group will be highly organized with an executive committee and various subcommittees. In others it will be more loosely organized with only ad hoc committees formed as the need arises. The youth group will be supported by youth sponsors, usually four to six adults appointed or elected by the youth or by the entire congregation. The sponsors serve terms of varying lengths, usually not less than two years.

Youth group will include all high school aged youth. Smaller congregations may choose to incorporate youth in grades 7 and 8 (junior high school) as well. Persons who have graduated from high school and remain in their home communities can be encouraged to continue to participate in youth group activities. Some congregations will develop a junior youth group for grades 7-8 youth and a senior youth group for grades 9-12 youth and post-highs, each with their own sponsors.

How often the youth group meets will vary considerably from congregation to congregation. In some, weekly meetings, often on a weeknight, will be planned. In others, the group will meet only once or twice a month.

The primary function of the youth group is to provide a setting where youth can gather with peers of the congregation who share similar values and experiences, for times of fun and fellowship, for study and discussion of a variety of issues, and for mutual support and encouragement in the Christian life. Youth may be introduced to new experiences through their youth group such as involvement with new cultural or economic groups through service activities. Developing and learning leadership skills is also an important purpose of youth group involvement.

An effective youth group will provide acceptance and affirmation for each group member. Consequently, programming that focuses on developing warm friendships among the youth of the congregation is of the greatest importance. It will help to develop the young person's social skills both through affirmation of the individual's contribution and sensitive confrontation of specific behaviors when needed.

Youth group programming will minimize competitive activities that make persons feel devalued and incapable. It will provide an atmosphere where the interests and abilities of each young person can be given expression and tested and a setting where ideas can be shared without fear of ridicule or put down. The following paragraphs list key youth group emphases:

1. *Many occasions for fun and fellowship.* Examples of activities that emphasize fun and fellowship include periods of time playing games that stress cooperation and avoid excessive competition, eating together as in "progressive meals," attending cultural, music, or athletic events followed by a snack together, weekend retreats or lock-ins, or times of just being together informally for a movie, conversation, or snack.

2. *Study and discussion of particular issues and concerns of young persons.* A curriculum or an elective study may be used and it may extend over a period of weeks as

part of the regular youth group meeting. Examples of such studies include dating and preparation for marriage, war and peace, family life concerns, or social and political issues like hunger, unemployment, or race relations. International and global issues can also be discussed. Using the Bible as a resource in these discussions will help youth understand how they can respond to these concerns as Christians.

In our discussion of the Sunday school we have noted that agenda more typical of youth group may take place during the Sunday school time. Where this is the case, special Bible studies or studies of beliefs and doctrines of the church, and church history could be planned for interested youth. Those who take part will likely have a higher degree of commitment and will give themselves to more serious study and preparation. These might be weeknight activities or held at another more convenient time.

3. *Involvement in mission and service ministries.* The youth group will plan for regular times of service to others in their own community and beyond. Every community offers a wide variety of possible service projects. Children, elderly persons and those with disabilities, persons living in crisis or in poverty—all represent possible mission and service opportunities in the home community. Reaching out to friends in school and welcoming them to participate in youth group and church activities is an important mission for youth.

Service and mission opportunities in locations away from home can also be arranged. These could be weekend or week-long projects. Disaster cleanup and repair, assisting with summer Bible school, and building renovation are examples of these special projects.

4. *Involvement with others from within the congregation.* To assure that the youth group is an integral part of the larger congregation, activities will be planned that bring together various elements and age groupings. For example, the youth group could plan activities such as

youth-senior citizen banquets, special programming for younger children, or evenings of informal fun and games for the entire congregation.

5. *Involvement with persons from other congregations.* Youth group programming will include activities that bring together youth from several or many congregations. This interaction will help youth keep their participation in the larger fellowship of believers, particularly within their own denomination, in focus. One youth group might invite another for an evening of social activities and worship. Youth groups will also want to participate as a group in district conference and churchwide youth activities such as camping, winter retreats, and youth conventions.

6. *Fund-raising activities.* The costs of youth group programming as outlined above will be funded partially through the congregational budget to which the youth will be encouraged to contribute. The remainder will be financed through special fund- raising projects of the youth group itself.

Catechism (instruction for baptism and church membership)

Baptism is the symbol of the youth's personal decision to follow Christ and unite formally with the church in membership. It is typically preceded by a time of formal instruction and preparation. In some congregations this is referred to as catechism. Others refer to it as instruction class.

Patterns for catechism vary from congregation to congregation. In some, all youth entering a designated grade, such as grade 9, enter catechism and work together through a study process that may last as long as two years. Others work with individuals. At the point an individual expresses interest in baptism and church membership, an individualized approach that may extend over several weeks or months is developed.

These two approaches represent extremes with many other patterns in between. Not only do congregations develop their own ways of teaching catechism, but what is taught varies a great deal, too. The denominational materials differ as well. The uniqueness of each congregation also provides important agenda for catechism instruction. Many pastors have developed their own unique approach to doing such instruction.

The age that young persons enter into catechism and baptism varies a great deal. The trend in some congregations is for youth to wait until their late teen years, while some others may baptize persons as young as ten or twelve years. Many persons would prefer an older age, perhaps near the time of graduation from secondary school. Baptism and formally joining the community of faith are preferable at this time because the young person, it is assumed, is ready to make adult decisions in other areas.

In a believers' church, the decision to enter into a period of catechism and request baptism should be voluntary, just as is the decision to unite with the church. If catechism class is for a particular age group, the decision to follow through with baptism must be made by the individual, as freely as possible from pressure to do it just because everyone else is doing so. The youth in instruction class must have the freedom to say no, or not yet, to baptism.

The content of catechism instruction, just as its pattern, varies in different congregations. The following list, though not exhaustive, suggests areas that might be included. In all the areas mentioned, the basic approach will be to help the young person express his or her understandings and to help expand those understandings where they seem incomplete. In most cases, this will involve a review of what has already been learned.

1. Reflection on how faith has developed, including the role of family and congregation in this development.

2. The meaning of being a Christian in today's world and what it means to take faith seriously in everyday living.

3. The meaning of baptism in the Anabaptist/believers' church tradition.

4. The place of the Bible in the Christian's experience and the role of other disciplines that help in living the Christian life.

5. The meaning of church membership, both historically and in the local congregation, including specific expectations and responsibilities of the members and how members can receive support and counsel through the church.

6. The ministry of the local congregation, its structure and organization, how it carries out its common life, including how it makes decisions, and how members can contribute their gifts through it.

7. Discussion of what it means to be Mennonite/Church of the Brethren, including discussion of its beliefs and doctrines, noting those held in common with all other Christians and where there are differences.

8. Specific planning for the baptismal service.

In each of the above areas the Bible will be the primary resource, although a curriculum may be used to guide and focus the learning. Learning from the experiences of persons who have committed themselves to Christ and the church, both contemporary and from church history, will be more effective than only having theoretical discussions.

The catechism class experience offers a unique opportunity for an adult in the congregation to develop a special supportive relationship with a young person, if such a mentoring relationship does not already exist. During the period of instruction, congregations may want to name a sponsor for each young person. They will meet regularly to discuss further the content introduced in the catechism class. Mentors can incorporate such discussions into their regular times together. In this way the baptismal candidates are given an additional means of discussing important concerns as well as having available the experience of another adult from the congregation.

Persons trained in spiritual direction offer a unique resource to youth preparing for baptism. Such persons can guide the young person to a deeper, more focused spirituality, helping the youth develop greater sensitivity to the longings of their soul, through careful listening and the development of helpful spiritual disciplines.

Mentoring relationships

The Integrated Congregational Youth Ministry includes two settings that build on one-to-one relationships. The first of these is the *mentoring relationship*. We will consider the second, *peer ministry*, in the next section.

One-to-one relationships offer a unique approach to youth ministry. They are increasingly important because of two major changes that have taken place in the past decade. First, youth in the church once found their best friends in the church. Today, however, most find their best friends in school as they participate together in sports, speech, drama, music, and a host of other school-planned social activities.

The most significant outcome of this change is that school friends often do not share the same beliefs and values. They may put more "strings" on the relationship. Such strings are typically related to performance. For example, the friendship will remain strong only as long as one continues to make a good contribution to the team or band or other activity. Or the friendship may suffer if a youth will not participate in all the activities of the group, especially if he or she will not state the reason for not joining in.

Church friends are more likely to give unconditional

friendship. There is less potential for conflict over what to do together because the values and beliefs are similar. In the accepting context of the group, youth are more free to report feelings, impressions, concerns, and ideas.

In urban areas it is even more difficult for the youth group to be the primary support group for the congregation's young persons. Living in many different parts of the city, the youth likely do not attend the same high school. Distances and transportation difficulties prevent regular meetings of the youth group. Consequently, the only time the youth of the congregation see each other is on Sunday morning. Building strong, supportive relationships among the youth is nearly impossible. This is true even in larger congregations that have plenty of youth—enough to have had an active youth group a decade ago.

The second major change that the church must face is the declining number of youth in general, and in congregations in particular. Some larger congregations are now experiencing what smaller congregations have always dealt with—having too few youth to have an active youth group. It has become necessary for these congregations to rethink their approach to youth ministry and look for other ways to minister to their youth.

Where congregations depend largely on the youth group as their youth ministry, the unconditional love and support that come from relationships between the generations may be limited or lost. One-to-one relationships can be a good way to provide for such support. Furthermore, one-to-one relationships enable congregations that do not have enough youth for a youth group to work with and support in intentional ways those youth they do have.

The mentoring relationship is especially useful in congregations in these circumstances. The mentoring relationship is an intentional, intergenerational relationship. It is intergenerational in that it makes an adult, usually of the same sex, available to each youth person. It is intentional in the sense that an adult commits her- or himself to caring for and walking with the youth during the high school years. In doing this, the adult will be a special resource as the young person works through decisions.

This adult mentor will help the young person reflect on past experiences and become aware of different possible ways to approach decisions. The two will engage in open dialogue on important concerns that might not be discussed elsewhere. These adult mentors can provide an open, supportive, unconditionally accepting relationship in congregations where this need cannot be met through the youth group.

In addition, congregations with active youth groups can find the one-to-one mentoring relationship useful. Mentors provide support outside of the youth group for working through particular concerns and issues that youth might be hesitant to raise in a group setting. Mentors thus provide more personal, individual support which sponsors may, for lack of time, find difficult to give.

The mentor will be careful not to be judgmental but will be free to sensitively raise questions regarding the youth's decision making. The mentor may be able to share how he or she made a similar decision at an earlier time.

The youth is matched with an adult in a process that involves both the youth and his or her parents. A good time to begin this relationship is at age twelve, although it can be initiated at any age. Some congregations start the mentoring program with young persons entering grade 7 and others wait until grade 9. Many of these relationships last in the formal sense through the end of high school. A youth can be matched with a new mentor if, for some reason, that seems best.

After being matched, the youth and mentor meet at least monthly for an extended, formal time together. Most mentoring pairs also talk informally in person or by telephone as the occasion permits. Much of what they do and talk about together arises out of the youth's interests and experiences. Times together may include a specific activity which the youth enjoys or it may be simply spending times together for a snack and talking about sports, fashions, school, family, friends, or whatever else interests the youth.

It is important that the mentor develop good listening skills because the youth must be at ease in order to share what may be causing pain or struggle. The mentor who listens well can help the youth work through problems and concerns and celebrate joys as well. The youth can gain a helpful perspective and learn to critique the wide range of the culture's messages that come daily. Doing this is the work of personal integration, bringing together and making sense out of life itself.

Some congregations may encourage their mentoring pairs to talk about special concerns in their times together. Or the youth and mentor may wish to use an outside resource, such as a book to study together, as a way to give more focus and purpose to their relationship. A book of mutual interest that both read prior to meeting can give them helpful discussion material. We have already noted the possible involvement of the mentor with the youth in the catechism process.

The mentoring relationship can be particularly appropriate when the youth is exploring occupational goals. Decision making in this area is highly personal as the youth builds on individual interests and abilities and seeks to discover a possible occupation. They can also consider what additional training beyond high school might be needed and where they might get such training.

Mentors can play a crucial role in helping youth consider what the implications of faith, values, relationships, and worldview are in choosing certain occupations. Mentors can also bring the resources of their own experiences to the young person and open the doors to the experience of others. Several helpful curriculum study guides are available for use in mentoring relationships on this topic. (See pages 124-125.)

There will also be times when all or a number of the mentoring pairs will meet together to work with specific concerns or issues. Group activities that are primarily social can help build relationships between younger youth and their mentors. The catechism class leader may want to include a time during the sessions for youth-mentor dialogue or focus questions for discussion at a later time.

The mentoring relationship can be an extremely useful youth ministry setting. But if it is to be useful to the fullest extent, it will require a high degree of commitment on the mentor's part. Mentors who commit themselves to such a relationship, but fail to follow though, are doing a great disservice to their youth. On the other hand, mentors who give themselves in an intentional, consistent relationship are contributing significantly to helping youth build solid foundations for significance.

Peer ministries

The second one-to-one relationship in the Integrated Congregational Youth Ministry can be referred to as peer helping or peer ministry. This setting helps youth develop special skills so that they can reach out and be of assistance to their peers beyond what even a close friendship can do. This approach has been pioneered by Dr. Barbara Varenhorst, a school psychologist in the public school system in Palo Alto, California. For a church which incorporates a strong emphasis on service to others, it is an approach that fits, with some adaptation, quite naturally for use in congregational youth ministry.

Peer helping consists of three specific components. Participants enter a period of (1) *training*, after which they may enter into a (2) *peer ministry assignment*. The final component is the arrangement for (3) *support* during their assignment. Youth become involved in the program on the basis of their interest and willingness to commit themselves to a time of serious training in building relationship skills. Part of this is a definite intention to attend every session of the training program. Let us look at each of the three components in greater detail.

1. *Training.* The young persons who enter the training program will follow carefully prepared curriculum that focuses on skills like meeting and communicating with new persons, asking questions that require responses beyond yes or no, and various other areas. The goal is to help a special caring relationship develop. The material will be covered in a specified number of weekly sessions or on a weekend retreat.

The training program is designed to prepare the participants for a peer ministry assignment. It also helps the participant know his or her limitations and when and where referrals can be made. Those who are trained will almost always experience significant personal growth. The training program is led by the program coordinator who has been trained for this purpose. The training program is designed to prepare the participants for a peer-helper assignment.

A training program of this nature almost always results in personal growth. Some who complete it, however, may not be ready for the helping role. Deciding whether a young person is ready for a peer-helper assignment is done in dialogue with the program coordinator.

2. *Ministry involvement.* One of the key tasks of the coordinator is to find places where those trained in peer helping can use their gifts. In the congregation this might be in helping younger persons find their way into the youth group and feel welcome within the larger congregation. This may involve contacts that encourage regular attendance at church and youth group functions. For example, the peer counselor would make certain that his or her peer would be able to get to youth group functions and take special interest in him or her there.

Another area where a peer counselor could be of service is in helping a junior high aged youth who is struggling academically. A little help from someone who can spend some time each week may get that person over some rough spots. It might be a peer mentoring role with a younger person who is finding the adjustment to junior high or secondary school difficult.

Ministry assignments do not always need to be with persons close in age to the one trained. Peer-helpers might be assigned for particular periods of time to assist a teacher of a younger Sunday school class. The person would work with an individual child who finds the class difficult for some reason. Another assignment might take the peer-helper into a retirement center or nursing facility to begin a special relationship with an elderly resident who receives few if any visitors.

In peer-helper assignments young persons commit themselves to regular contact with individuals to whom they are assigned. Such contacts include checking in, assisting as appropriate, and especially listening.

3. *Support.* An important part of a peer-helping program is the ongoing support the peer-helper receives in the ministry assignment. Some form of support must be set up to which peer-helpers can bring concerns, frustrations, and struggles. It will also be a place to celebrate the growth, both of the peer-helper and the one being helped.

At a minimum, a monthly meeting of all those having assignments should be held. Here peer-helpers can come to report on their relationship and receive counsel from the group. Alternative approaches they might use in their relationship if things are not going well can be discussed. It might also involve a program of advanced training for interested persons.

A peer-helping program will demand a high degree of commitment on the part of the youth who become involved as well as on those adults who give leadership to it. Some youth will not be sufficiently disciplined for such involvement. These persons should not be encouraged to participate without carefully assessing their willingness to carry through.

For some, such a commitment could be a next step in their own faith journey. But, as in mentoring, those who make such a commitment, even after completing the training program, to walk with another person but fail to follow through do a great deal of harm.

Peer helping can be an extremely effective and concrete means of carrying out our youth ministry purpose of being an expression of God's love in the world.

Family life

We have come to expect a certain amount of tension between parents and their daughters and sons during the teenage years. Interestingly, both are concerned with finding a sense of purpose and meaning in life. In each case, this concern is worked at quite differently and this can often be a source of tension. Mom and Dad, on the one hand, need to deal with the reality that they are entering what will likely be the last major productive phase of their lives. They are concerned with leaving a legacy in their world. Having accumulated many things—both in terms of memories, possessions, and experiences, they are ready to settle down and "stay put."

Teens, on the other hand, look for purpose and meaning differently. They are idealistic and are trying out a wide variety of options for their involvement in the future. They are ready to explore various lifestyle possibilities. Some will want to travel and explore the world and see how other people live. They are not particularly concerned about settling down but rather want to be free to fly on their own. Independence, especially from their parents, is a key concern of many youth.

Furthermore, we find in our congregations a wide variety of families. Many youth may still come from the traditional two-parent family, but more and more are from one-parent and blended families.

A healthy family life has a significant impact on the attitude of the young person in all areas of life, including how they feel about faith and church. On the other hand, significant tension and conflict in the family will affect youth's attitudes, including those that lead to a feeling of significance. Tension and conflict will also contribute to negative feelings about church and even withdrawal from other youth ministry settings.

Ministry to the young person in each of the settings that we have already described can contribute to healthy family life. Parents will find mentoring relationships to be very supportive. Youth will often find in their mentors a more objective understanding of the family situation. A caring, accepting youth group can provide a young person with a comfortable place when tensions arise at home. Youth group discussions about family life can also be very helpful.

An Integrated Congregational Youth Ministry will include an emphasis on family life separate from the other settings. There will be in the congregation's program at least one major annual emphasis on strengthening the family. Parent-teen or teen-sibling relationships can be the focus of this annual emphasis. It can also take the shape of preparing families with soon-to-be teenagers for that time.

Such an effort should be planned in close consultation with youth leaders in order to focus on concerns of the youth as well as the parents. The following ways illustrate how to strengthen family life through an Integrated Congregational Youth Ministry.

1. *Teen-parent retreat.* A teen-parent retreat is a time when teens and their parents can be together in a retreat setting and where they can give attention to their relationship. Such a retreat might be planned for an entire weekend, a Friday evening- Saturday, or Sunday afternoon-evening time frame. Resource persons can be secured to help the group process issues like communication, sexuality, peer pressure, and others.

2. *Sunday school electives.* Leaders might plan Sunday school electives that focus on issues of concern to families. For example, classes might be designed to help parents relate to their children. Such classes might be intergenera-

tional or only for parents and other adults.

3. *Including teens in small groups.* Where congregations encourage members to be part of a small group, teens could be encouraged to participate in their parents' small group. Should this not seem feasible on an ongoing basis, a block of small group meetings could be designated for participation by teens. Such meetings would likely emphasize fellowship, but topics that would be of interest to teens and adults alike could be discussed.

4. *Encouraging parent involvement in marriage enrichment programs.* Various marriage enrichment activities and events are often planned within congregations or on a conference or churchwide basis. The congregation could help parents become involved in such programs through budgeting the costs for a given number of couples to attend such an event. Provision should be made for each set of parents to participate in at least one marriage enrichment experience during the teen years of their children.

5. *Parent support groups.* Tensions in teen-parent relationships are normal in the experience of most families. In some cases, these normal tensions are heightened by unacceptable behavior, getting in with the wrong crowd, or even scrapes with the law. Whatever the level of stress, many parents would find significant help in a setting where they can freely confess their struggles, be accepted no matter how they think they may have failed, and receive counsel for their continuing attempts at building healthy relationships. For some parents and their families professional counseling may be essential. But for many others, congregational support groups where parents can find help and hope can be very helpful. Such groups might be ongoing or for specific periods of time such as a weekly meeting for a designated time.

Chapter 10: THE YOUTH MINISTRY TEAM: putting feet on the Integrated Congregational Youth Ministry

Congregations using the Integrated Congregational Youth Ministry will appoint a ministry team whose purpose it will be to develop, oversee, and carry out the total ongoing youth ministry of the congregation.

We have noted that the typical approach in congregations has been to place the primary responsibility for youth ministry on the youth group and the sponsors. Many of these persons have given far beyond what other volunteers give, and in many cases that ministry has born much fruit. On the other hand, we have also noted the increasing difficulties that many sponsors face in their task.

Those congregations using the Integrated Congregational Youth Ministry will appoint a *youth ministry team* whose purpose will be to develop, oversee, and carry out the total ongoing youth ministry. The team will include representatives of those groups most directly interested in the youth and those who have specific responsibility for leadership of the youth ministry program. These may include:

- pastor (or youth pastor or pastoral team member whose responsibilities include youth ministry)
- elder or deacon (a representative of the congregation's board of elders or deacons)

- parents (two parents, both of whom are parents of teens)
- youth (two or three carefully selected youth leaders)
- adult leaders (those persons who are appointed to serve as adult leaders of the programs of the various settings selected for youth ministry. Included here would be the youth group sponsors, the youth Sunday school class teacher, mentor program coordinator, peer-helper program coordinator)

Other persons who might be appointed or who might be a resource to the team include a person from the administrative group responsible for youth ministry, such as the Christian education commission, and a representative from the congregation's family life committee.

The youth ministry team will be appointed by the congregation's board of elders/deacons or the church council in counsel with the various groups represented. For example, the youth should be given the opportunity to select their representative. Parents may also wish to be involved in the selection of the parent representatives.

The team will meet at least quarterly to give direction for the overall youth ministry of the congregation. Specific areas of responsibility include:

1. *Determining needs.* A critical responsibility of the youth ministry team is to give careful thought to the individual and collective needs of the youth of the congregation. Initially this means making a list of all the youth. This might be done by drawing a large map with the church's meetinghouse in the center and putting each youth's name approximately where he or she lives. Helpful personal information could be listed beside each name: where they attend school; place in the family; and church, school, and community involvements. Concerns of particular interest to the youth can also be noted if these are known.

Such a map is intended for the youth ministry team only, and is not to be displayed on the youth minister's or the congregational bulletin board. It will provide a means of getting a handle on the needs of each young person in the congregation. The team can decide which of the youth ministry goals to focus on and how these will be placed and sequenced in the larger youth ministry program.

The team will be concerned about planning a balanced program. It will focus on the obvious or felt needs of the youth that are listed in the information on the map. The team will also be ready to address those goals that may not be of obvious concern to the youth. For example, learning to know the Bible may not emerge from the map as a top priority concern of many of the youth. However, from the congregation's viewpoint, it is of great importance.

2. *Settings.* Many congregations may not use all of the youth ministry settings listed in chapter 9 in their program. Some congregations will, but others will need to select the best settings depending on the needs of their youth and the resources of the congregation. It will be the responsibility of the youth ministry team to carefully assess this and choose those settings which will provide a balanced ministry.

Some of the settings are, in a sense, not optional. For example, congregational worship and family life exist regardless of the youth ministry program. Strengthening ministry in both of these areas should, therefore, be given highest priority.

The size of the congregation will influence somewhat the settings that will be chosen. Small congregations, for example, may wish to emphasize most strongly mentoring relationships simply because they do not have enough youth for an active youth group. Larger congregations with a less active or ambitious youth group program may also choose to emphasize mentoring. Where the youth group has been effective, the team can give suggestions for strengthening it.

Any combination of the settings can work in a congregation. The important thing is that they be chosen deliberately and then be given solid support.

3. *Content and focus.* The needs of the group and the

116

goals for the Integrated Congregational Youth Ministry program will provide a framework for deciding how to make the best use of each of the settings. Selecting curriculum for Sunday school, for instance, could be done by the team taking into consideration what else is happening in the youth world. A balanced program will include not only those things that youth typically want to talk about or do. It will also bring into the program some content growing out of the goals that may not be otherwise touched upon.

The team will help the teachers of the youth Sunday school class determine whether the class time should be spent in relationship building or in structured education. If it is the latter, the team will work with the teachers to determine whether the curriculum recommended by the denomination is appropriate for the youth, given their needs and level of interest and commitment. They will give ideas for adapting the denominational curriculum or for selecting another if necessary.

The team can also assist the pastor in developing content for catechism. It will determine what, if any, resource will be made available to mentors. The youth group leaders and sponsors will want to work with the entire youth group to decide programming in youth group, taking into consideration what is taking place in each of the other settings. The team can also be a sounding board for the sponsors and youth leaders as they plan activities that will involve significant time commitment and major expense, such as attending the churchwide youth conference or taking a week-long service trip.

4. *Budget.* Another important task of the youth ministry team deals with funding the program. Traditionally the youth have raised money through all sorts of projects to fund all the activities of the youth group. With additional settings now requiring possible funding, the team will need to think carefully about how costs in these settings can be covered. In a more general way, this task also relates to teaching stewardship to the youth of the congregation.

The team may ask that the youth group continue to do

its fundraisers, working carefully with them to determine how much they can be expected to raise. The youth group may also contribute from its funds for costs related to other youth ministry settings or these may be covered through a line item in the congregational budget.

Some youth groups have begun tithing a portion of the funds they raise to the congregational budget as a symbolic means of recognizing their relationship to the congregation. Or, they may undertake special fundraisers to assist when special needs arise. For example, one youth group, after a tragic fire destroyed their building, decided to clean the charred bricks to sell as mementos of the burned building, but more importantly of the congregation's experiences in it over the years. The money they raised was contributed to the building fund for a new church meetinghouse.

A few congregations are including the entire youth program (including youth group expenses) in the congregation's budget. This is done to reduce the heavy emphasis on fund raising in the youth group and to free them for other activities such as study or service. It is also seen as a practical way to tie the youth into the life of the congregation. Any funds raised by the youth group become part of the congregation's budget and costs of all youth ministry activities are paid through it. Youth are strongly encouraged to pledge a tithe of their personal income as contributions to the congregation.

5. *Support for the youth ministry leaders.* I have already noted that the youth ministry team may serve as a sounding board for the youth group sponsors and leaders as they work with the youth group. The team can do this for all persons who give leadership to any part of the program. It will be open to hearing any concerns and problems that come up. It will want to hear the joys and particular experiences that have resulted in growth for the youth.

One particular way that the team can support those in leadership is to be aware of leadership-training events to which the various persons go. Such programs are often offered by the district conference youth ministry staff person. Some parachurch organizations also provide helpful in-service training programs. Funds for persons to attend such training events should be included in the budget.

6. *Evaluation.* Another important task of the youth ministry team will be to evaluate the youth ministry program. This will include evaluation of each of the separate settings. Its larger focus will be to determine whether the program as it is being carried out is helping youth *be and become unique expressions of God's love in the world.* This is, as we have stated before, our vision and purpose for the Integrated Congregational Youth Ministry.

This evaluation will be ongoing in the dialogue within the youth ministry team. Finding ways to get direct responses from the youth will also be essential. This might be through a questionnaire or dialogue with a representative group of youth. It may also be helpful to get an outside resource person, such as a district conference or churchwide youth ministry staff member, to give some additional assistance. The evaluation process is important because it will be the basis on which new program directions can be established and content can be reorganized.

7. *Reporting to the congregation.* A final task of the youth ministry team is to inform the larger congregation of what is happening in the youth ministry. They may give brief informational "spots" during the congregation's sharing time on Sunday morning. They may write a brief or a longer article on the youth ministry page in the monthly congregational newsletter. They may plan a special service in which the youth group reports on its experience on the annual service trip or at the churchwide youth conference.

The congregation that is a community of faith will be deeply interested in what is happening in the youth ministry. They want to know because the youth are part of them. Through being informed, the congregation will be able to more fully take ownership in this important program.

CONCLUSION

The word *success* has occasionally been used in this book. While I usually noticed when it crept in, I recognize that thinking in terms of success is a part of our success-oriented, Western thinking and culture.

Certainly success in youth ministry is something we want to strive for. However, *faithfulness* is far more important than success in youth ministry. An orientation that emphasizes success frequently results in feelings of failure. This is because such an orientation tends to be short-term, looking constantly for signs that are marks of success. Sadly, it gives in too quickly when those signs are not there.

An orientation to faithfulness, on the other hand, hangs in there over the long haul. There is celebration when a young person expresses God's love in her or his world. And, disappointments will not give in to failure. Rather, they are seen as times to reflect and evaluate, and possibly give rise to renewal and to strengthening of commitment to even greater faithfulness. A youth ministry leader's greatest joy may come much later in life when a person in the thirty- to forty-year age group contributes significantly to building God's kingdom. The leader may then realize that he or she touched that life as a teenager and may have had a small part in preparing that person for ministry.

The first step in faithfulness is the development of a blueprint for youth ministry in your congregation. The dictionary defines *blueprint* as a "detailed plan of action." The purpose of our work in this book is to provide an approach on which to develop a blueprint—your own plan of action for youth ministry in your congregation. It is an approach that takes advantage of every opportunity in the life of the congregation where it touches the lives of its youth.

Developing a youth ministry blueprint is in many respects similar to developing a blueprint or plan for constructing a house. Such a plan has a variety of rooms—kitchen, living room, bedroom, bath, and others. Each room has its own special function and features. Each provides a setting for many memorable family and personal activities.

For too long it has been assumed that youth ministry will take place in only one room, that is, the youth group. There are other rooms but leaders forget about them or leaders do not believe they have any potential for helping youth shape their identity and build their lives. We must understand the uniqueness of each young person and their task of shaping their identity and building their life. If we understand this, we will know that some youth will find themselves more at ease in certain rooms and less comfortable in others.

A blueprint for youth ministry that takes advantage of all the settings in the congregation where the lives of youth are touched will faithfully reach out and respond to their uniqueness. It will do so with the clear purpose of seeing each youth shape an identity and build a life focused in being and becoming an expression of God's love in the world.

The blueprint that is developed for your congregation's youth ministry will determine which "room"—setting—will be included in the youth ministry program. You can then seek out the needed resources to carry out the specific plans. Some of these already exist in your congregation. Others are available through the youth ministry offices of your district or conference. Some new ones may need to be developed. Indeed, the denominations that cooperated in the writing of this book will continue to work together to develop resources for the various settings in the next years to service the Integrated Congregational Youth Ministry as described in this book.

Your denominational youth ministry offices also stand ready to assist you in carrying out your congregational youth ministry blueprint. You may feel free to write to any of the following offices:

Youth Ministries Office
Church of the Brethren General Offices
1451 Dundee Avenue
Elgin, IL 60120

Secretary of Youth Education
Commission on Education
General Conference Mennonite Church
722 Main St., Box 347
Newton, KS 67114-0347

Congregational Youth Ministries
Mennonite Board of Congregational Ministries
Box 1245
Elkhart, IN 46515-1245

In many congregations youth ministry is very much like the burning grocery store described in chapter 1. It is burning! But even though this is the case, we need not stand back and wring our hands hopelessly. Nor do we need to only wish nostalgically for the "good old days" when all seemed to be well in youth ministry. Rather, with God's help, we can see beyond the flames an opportunity for rebuilding lives and programs. We can reach out in caring and loving ways to every young person in the congregation.

Our ultimate vision is that young persons throughout the church are and become expressions of God's love where they are. If this is to happen we must walk with them in such a way that each one will decide to form an identity and build a life which will be seen in decisions that truly reflect the image of God as God created them. This is no small task. But it is one that has been entrusted to us. We can, with God's help, be faithful in it and in so doing, lead them to the source of true significance.

FOR FURTHER READING

Part I

Posterski, Donald C. *Friendship: A Window on Ministry to Youth.* Scarborough, Ont.: Project Teen Canada, 1985.

Strommen, Merton P. *Five Cries of Youth.* San Francisco: Harper and Row, 1979.

Warren, Michael. *Youth and the Future of the Church.* New York: The Seabury Press, 1982.

Warren, Michael. *Youth, Gospel, Liberation.* San Francisco: Harper and Row, 1987.

Part II

Irwin, Paul B. *The Care and Counseling of Youth in the Church.* Philadelphia: Fortress Press, 1975.

Jeschke, Marlin. *Believer's Baptism for Children of the Church.* Scottdale, Pa.: Herald Press, 1983.

Jones, Stephen D. *Faith Shaping.* Valley Forge: Judson Press, 1980.

Ng, David. *Youth in the Community of Disciples.* Valley Forge: Judson Press, 1984.

Martin, Maurice. *Identity and Faith.* Scottdale, Pa.: Herald Press, 1981.

Martin, Maurice, with Helen Reusser. *In the Midst of the Congregation.* Scottdale, Pa.: Mennonite Publishing House, 1983.

Part III

Congregational worship

Lehn, Cornelia. *Involving Children and Youth in Congregational Worship.* Newton, Kans.: Faith and Life Press and Scottdale, Pa.: Mennonite Publishing House, 1982.

Youth Sunday school

Cummings, Mary Lou, and Helmut Harder. *Called to Teach Youth.* Scottdale, Pa.: Mennonite Publishing House and Newton, Kans.: Faith and Life Press, 1981.

Youth group

Griffin, Em. *Getting Together: A Guide for Good Groups.* Downers Grove, Il.: Intervarsity Press, 1982.

Robbins, Duffy. *Programming to Build Disciples.* Victor Books, 1987.

Rydberg, Denny. *Building Community in Youth Groups.* Loveland, Colo.: Group Books, 1985.

Schultz, Thom, and Joani Schultz. *Involving Youth in Youth Ministry.* Loveland, Colo.: Group Books, 1987.

Catechism

Bauman, Kenneth. *Invitation to Life.* Newton: Faith and Life Press, 1986.

Erb, Paul. *We Believe.* Scottdale: Herald Press, 1969.

Harder, Helmut. *Guide to Faith.* Newton: Faith and Life Press, 1979.

Kehler, Larry. *Focus on Faith.* Newton: Faith and Life Press, 1978.

Keller, Frank R. *Preparation for Covenant Life.* Newton: Faith and Life Press, 1979.

Krabill, Russell. *Beginning the Christian Life.* Scottdale: Herald Press, 1988.

Martin, Ernest. *Experiencing Christ in the Church.* Scottdale: Mennonite Publishing House, 1971.

Martin, Ernest. *Preparing for Church Membership.* Scottdale: Mennonite Publishing House, 1971.

Stutzman, Ervin R. *Being God's People.* Scottdale: Mennonite Publishing House, 1985.

Waltner, James H. *This We Believe.* Newton: Faith and Life Press, 1968.

Yoder, Bruce. *Choose Life.* Scottdale: Mennonite Publishing House, 1984.

Mentoring relationships

Bingham, Mindy, Judy Edmondson, and Sandy Stryker. *Challenge: A Young Man's Journal for Self-awareness and Personal Planning.* Santa Barbara, Calif.: Advocacy Press, 1984.

Bingham, Mindy, Judy Edmondson, and Sandy Stryker.

Choices: A Teen Woman's Journal for Self-awareness and Personal Planning. Santa Barbara, Calif.: Advocacy Press, 1983.

Welty, Lavon J., ed. *The Life Planning Program.* Published by the youth ministries office of the Mennonite Board of Congregational Ministries, Box 1245, Elkhart, IN 46515.

Peer ministries

Myrick, Robert D., and Tom Erney. *Caring and Sharing: Becoming a Peer Facilitator.* Minneapolis: Educational Media Corporation, 1984.

Myrick, Robert D., and Tom Erney. *Youth Helping Youth, a Handbook for Training Peer Facilitators.* Minneapolis: Educational Media Corporation, 1984.

Varenhorst, Barbara B. *Curriculum Guide for Student Peer Counseling Training.* Palo Alto, Calif.: Barbara B. Varenhorst, 1980.

Varenhorst, Barbara B., and Lee Sparks. *Training Teenagers for Peer Ministry.* Loveland, Colo.: Group Books, 1988.

Family life

Strommen, Merton P., and A. Irene Strommen. *Five Cries of Parents.* San Francisco: Harper and Row, 1985.

ABOUT THE AUTHOR

Lavon J. Welty was born near Wakarusa, Indiana, in 1943. He has lived in Elkhart County, Indiana, most of his life. He spent two years, 1963 to 1965, in international voluntary service under the Mennonite Central Committee (MCC) in Burundi, Africa, and served on the MCC headquarters staff in Akron, Pennsylvania, from 1968 to 1975.

Welty is married to Carol (Garber) Welty. They have two daughters, Andrea and Renetta. He graduated from Goshen College, Goshen, Indiana, in 1968 with an undergraduate degree in English. He also graduated from Goshen Biblical Seminary in 1979 with a Master of Divinity degree.

Welty's involvement in youth ministry began in 1975 when he became half-time youth minister for the Indiana-Michigan Conference of the Mennonite Church. In 1977 he accepted half-time employment with the Mennonite Board of Congregational Ministries (MBCM) as youth ministries staff person. He continued with both half-time positions until 1981, when the position with MBCM became full-time. He continues to serve in that position.

His avocational interests include bicycling and bicycle repair, woodworking, gardening and puttering around the house, knitting, and counted cross-stitch. He is becoming increasingly acquainted with the capabilities of his personal computer. The Weltys are active members of the Southside Fellowship congregation in Elkhart, Indiana, where Lavon serves as congregational treasurer, as a member of the worship committee, and, on occasion, as worship leader.